Stylistic variation in prehistoric ceramics

NEW STUDIES IN ARCHAEOLOGY

Stylistic variation in prehistoric ceramics

Design analysis in the American Southwest

STEPHEN PLOG

Department of Anthropology
University of Virginia

CAMBRIDGE UNIVERSITY PRESS

CAMBRIDGE
LONDON   NEW YORK   NEW ROCHELLE
MELBOURNE   SYDNEY

Published by the Press Syndicate of the University of Cambridge
The Pitt Building, Trumpington Street, Cambridge CB2 1RP
32 East 57th Street, New York, NY 10022, USA
296 Beaconsfield Parade, Middle Park, Melbourne 3206, Australia

First published 1980

Printed in the United States of America
Typeset by Huron Valley Graphics, Ann Arbor, Michigan
Printed and bound by the Hamilton Printing Company, Rensselaer,
New York

Library of Congress Cataloging in Publication Data

Plog, Stephen.

Stylistic variation in prehistoric ceramics.

(New studies in archaeology)

A revision of the author's thesis, University of
Michigan.

Bibliography: p.

1. Indians of North America – Southwest, New –
Antiquities. 2. Indians of North America – Southwest,
New – Pottery. 3. Indians of North America – Arizona –
Chevelon Valley – Antiquities. 4. Indians of North
America – Arizona – Chevelon Valley – Pottery. 5. South-
west, New – Antiquities. 6. Arizona – Antiquities.
7. Chevelon Valley, Ariz. – Antiquities. 8. Archaeology –
Methodology. 9. Culture diffusion. I. Title.
II. Series.
E78.S7P56 1980 979.1 79–23326
ISBN 0 521 22581 7

Contents

Preface

The analysis of stylistic variation on prehistoric artifacts has been a major component of archaeological research for decades, and the amount of literature that has been generated is immense. It would be extremely difficult for a single monograph to discuss all of the different issues that have been raised concerning stylistic variation and this study does not attempt to do so. Rather, it is an attempt to deal with one primary topic, the explanation of patterns of stylistic variation, which I feel has not received enough attention in previous analyses, particularly many that have been carried out in the last two decades.

Many types of inferences about the past and several methods of measuring characteristics of prehistoric human adaptive systems are based on patterns of stylistic variation and on assumptions about the factors which cause that variation. However, these assumptions are oversimplified in many instances and have not been adequately tested. Given this problem and the importance of patterns of stylistic variation in archaeological inferences, we must begin to try to understand the full range of factors that determine degrees and patterns of stylistic variation rather than to assume that these factors are already known. This study is an attempt at an initial step in that direction. It examines the extent to which change in stylistic attributes over time, the exchange of goods, the movement of people, and the association of stylistic attributes with the form of artifacts can explain ceramic design variation in one area of the American Southwest. In addition, the extent to which alternative theories of stylistic variation can account for spatial and temporal patterns in design variation in the American Southwest is addressed.

While this study is based on the analysis of a specific type of data from a specific area, I feel that the results of the research should be relevant to those interested in the analysis of stylistic variation on other types of artifacts from other areas of the world. In particular, the results have implications for a variety of methods that have been used to infer characteristics of prehistoric human interaction and social organization from patterns of stylistic variation.

Numerous individuals deserve thanks for their help in completing the research discussed in this study. First, David Braun, Genevieve Jones, Cay Loria, Laura Mason, and Christine Rudecoff, then of the University of Michigan, participated in the collection of data during the summer of 1974. In addition, several individuals from the State University of New York at Binghamton under the direction of Dr. Fred Plog also assisted in the data collection. Of these individuals, Bruce Donaldson, Margie Green, Patricia Rubertone, Isolde Wait, and Walter Wait deserve special thanks. Richard I. Ford, then my dissertation chairman, also assisted in the initial stages of the fieldwork.

Analysis of the data during the 1974–75 academic year was done with the help of Kurt Anschuetz, Mike Hambacher, Laura Mason, Frank Peryea, Diane Phelps, Christine Rudecoff, and Ellen Zak. Christine Rudecoff, in particular, deserves special thanks for her work on the preliminary design analysis. The petrographic analysis of the Chevelon ceramics was done by Elizabeth Garrett of the Department of Geology at Western Michigan University. She worked long hours making thin sections and doing the superb analysis described in this study.

This manuscript is a revised version of my doctoral dissertation. Richard I. Ford, Kent V. Flannery, John D. Nystuen, Robert E. Whallon, and Henry T. Wright, members of my dissertation committee, all provided invaluable comments on the dissertation proposal and on drafts and the final copy of the dissertation itself. George J. Gumerman, Fred Plog, and David Wilcox also read drafts of the dissertation and provided useful comments. Kent Flannery, Richard Ford, and Fred Plog also deserve special thanks for their guidance throughout my undergraduate and graduate years. Finally, my thinking on a number of the issues discussed in this study has been influenced by many long talks with David Braun and Alan Zarky.

A dissertation improvement grant (GS-42783) from the National Science Foundation made possible the collection of most of the data used in this study. A grant from the Graduate Student Research Fund at the University of Michigan in 1973 aided the formulation of the dissertation. Finally, the National Science Foundation provided a graduate fellowship to support my first years in graduate school. I am grateful for all this support.

I also want to thank Lindsay Catlin who typed the final manuscript and drafted Figures 7.1, 7.2, and 8.1 and Jean Baker who drafted Figures 1.1–5.1.

S.P.

I

Introduction to the problem

Studies of stylistic variation in prehistoric artifacts have played an important role in archaeological research since the beginning of the discipline. A variety of different types of studies have been done using a number of different methods and types of artifacts. The purpose of the majority of these studies, however, can be placed in one of two categories. First, the largest amount of research has concentrated on the *discovery and description of stylistic change through time in order to date sites*. Using sets of artifacts from stratigraphic sequences or from dated deposits for temporal control, it has been established in many areas that stylistic attributes changed through time. Early examples of such studies include the excavations of Kidder (1931, 1972) and Nelson (1916) in the American Southwest, Ford (1935) in the southeastern United States, Gamio (1913) and Vaillant (1930, 1931) in the Valley of Mexico, Bennett (1934) in Bolivia, and innumerable studies in Europe where stratigraphic excavations first were used as an important means of establishing temporal sequences. Such studies have continued to be important as a means of establishing new sequences, verifying old ones, or developing methods of making more precise estimates of occupation dates [e.g., the research of Drennan (1976) in the Valley of Oaxaca, Mexico, Snarkis (1976) in Costa Rica, and Thomas and others (1976) in Luxembourg].

The success of such studies led to the widespread use of stylistic attributes, such as types of ceramic designs or characteristics of projectile points, as *index fossils* (Colton and Hargrave 1937:17) for the dating of sites. In the American Southwest, for example, Martin and Plog (1973:252) have noted that within the ceramic wares defined by Colton (1955), 75 percent of the distinctions between the pottery types of different time periods are based on differences in stylistic attributes such as design elements or design layouts.

The second type of stylistic analysis has become particularly common in the last few decades and has concentrated on *stylistic variation through space rather than variation through time*. Specifically, such studies have attempted to infer characteristics of prehistoric social organization or interaction by measuring different aspects of stylistic variation. Two such aspects have been emphasized: (1) the similarity of stylistic attributes in different areas of a site or at different sites within a region and (2) the degree of homogeneity in the stylistic elements from a single site or within a region. These studies have been based on the assumption that the degree to which designs are shared by or diffuse between individuals, social segments, or villages is directly proportional to the amount of interaction between the units (Englebrecht 1974:53; Fry and Cox 1974:222; Kay 1975:64, 69–70; Longacre 1970:27–8; Pollnac and Rowlett 1977:170; Redman 1977:51 and 1978:172–3, 175; Whallon 1968:223). Given this assumption and others concerning the deposition of the ceramic material, the sex of the potters, and the importance of the link between mother and daughter in the daughter's learning of designs [see Baldwin (1975), S. Plog (1976a), and Schiffer (1976:22–5) for a more detailed discussion of the assumption], it has been argued that the greater the interaction between units, the higher will be the stylistic similarity between units and the lower the degree of stylistic homogeneity within sites. In contrast, if interaction is minimal and the stylistic traditions of individuals or social units are not shared to any extent, the lower will be the stylistic similarity between units and the higher will be the degree of homogeneity within units.

Based on this argument, some studies have attempted to isolate spatial units within an area in which the variation in the stylistic attributes present within the units is low relative to the variation between units or the degree of stylistic similarity within units is higher than the similarity between units. The spatial units which have been isolated have been interpreted as supracommunities or communities (Pollnac and Rowlett 1977), as groups of villages cooperating economically and ritually (Longacre 1964a), or as residence units within villages (Clemen 1976; Gerald 1975; Hill 1970; Longacre 1970). Others have used the same assumptions already outlined to describe the intensity of interaction between communities by measuring the degree of design variation within communities (Connor 1968; Englebrecht 1971, 1974; Leone 1968; McPherron 1967; Whallon 1968) or through quantification of the degree of stylistic similarity between villages (Englebrecht 1974, 1979; Fry and Cox 1974; Kay 1975; Tuggle 1970). Connor (1968), Leone (1968), and McPherron (1967:298) suggested that interaction intensities were determined by community marital rules, either virilocality versus uxorilocality or endogamy versus exogamy, while Engelbrecht (1974) has discussed the importance of increased rates of trade on interaction and stylistic variation.

Such studies have been made in a number of different areas, but are most numerous in analysis of North American prehistory. Studies focusing on stylistic similarity include the research of Longacre (1964a, 1970), Hill (1970), Cook (1970), Tuggle (1970), Wiley (1971), Gerald (1975), Hanson (1975), Clemen (1976), Redman (1978), Washburn (1977, 1978), Washburn and Matson (1980), and Kintigh (1979) in the American Southwest and Whallon (1969), Engelbrecht (1974, 1979), and Kay (1975) in the midwestern or northeastern United States. The work of Connor (1968) and Leone (1968) in the American Southwest and McPherron (1967), Whallon (1968, 1969), Engelbrecht (1971, 1974), and Braun (1977) in the midwestern or northeastern United States are examples of studies measuring stylistic homogeneity.

Outside of North American research, relatively few such analyses have been made. In the Old World, examples of studies of stylistic similarity for the purpose of inferring prehistoric organization or interaction include Pollnac and Rowlett's (1977) attempt to isolate communities and supracommunities using stylistic data from Marnian sites of the La Tene Ia period in Western Europe, Voss's (1976) research on intercommunity interaction in northwestern Europe from 2900 to 2200 B.C., and Redman's (1978) and Rubertone's (1978) analyses of organization and ceramic variation in the Moroccan site of Qsar es-Seghir. In Mesoamerica, Pyne's (1976) study of ceramic design distributions within three Formative (1150–650 B.C.) communities in the Valley of Oaxaca in Mexico, my analysis (1976b) of intersite stylistic similarities in the same area, and a study of interaction and stylistic similarities in the Tikal, Guatemala, region (Fry and Cox 1974) also are examples of the type of study just described. Although the number of these studies done using materials from areas outside of North America is small, many comparisons of stylistic similarities and differences between different regions, rather than individual sites, have been based implicitly on the same principle as the subregional studies listed here, as Flannery (1976:253) has argued. Statements such as the following are typical of such studies: "similar designs on pottery and textiles in the Interlocking and Recuoid cultures indicate that cultural relations existed between them" (Strong and Evans 1952:244).

The two general types of studies of stylistic variation described have been important for two reasons. First, artifact types, often distinguished by stylistic attributes, are the major analytical unit used by archaeologists in dating sites in many areas. Since the estimation of site dates is a prerequisite of most archaeological research, the knowledge that stylistic attributes changed through time has been and remains important. Second, the study of stylistic variation in order to infer characteristics of prehistoric organization and interaction has increased in importance as archaeologists have become more concerned with explaining prehistoric culture change. Many anthropologists have argued that culture change must be understood in terms of a society's adaptation to its physical and social environment. Yet, as Kushner (1970) and Flannery (1972) have argued, emphasis by archaeologists on the natural environment has exceeded emphasis on the social environment. This is a result of a lack of methods for measuring interaction between communities or for isolating sets and hierarchies of interaction units among or within villages. If the method recounted here can aid in the measurement of these aspects of the social environment, it will contribute significantly to our ability to describe and explain prehistoric culture change. Thus, studies of stylistic variation have provided and, in the future, may continue to provide important archaeological information.

Problems in the use of stylistic variation
While the different types of stylistic analyses have been and continue to be important to archaeologists, they conflict in their interpretations of stylistic variation. One interpretation views stylistic attributes as primarily varying temporally. The other interpretation views designs as primarily varying spatially. To accommodate this contradiction, most studies assume implicitly that stylistic change is sporadic, with periods of stability followed by rapid change. Stylistic characteristics are used to date sites according to periods of time or phases, emphasizing the temporal aspect of style variation; but within phases, stylistic change over time is assumed to be minimal and spatial patterns of stylistic variation are stressed. However, few if any studies have tested this assumed pattern of stylistic change. Given that the two primary interpretations of stylistic variation may be contradictory, we must ask whether there are problems with either of the interpretations.

First, are there problems with the use of designs to date sites? The series of studies by Deetz and Dethlefsen (Deetz 1968a; Deetz and Dethlefsen 1965, 1967; Dethlefsen and Deetz 1966) indicate definite problems. Their analysis of motifs carved on eighteenth and nineteenth century gravestones in New England revealed variation through space in the date of the initial appearance of designs and in the date of the highest relative frequency of designs because of factors such as distance from Boston where some motifs first occurred, the rate of religious change over space, and changes in subsistence bases and market orientations. Their analysis also demonstrated that the motifs changed continuously over time rather than sporadically. In a second study, Martin and Plog's (1973:257) analysis of Breternitz's dates for Southwestern ceramic types suggested that "the rate of adoption of artifacts including pottery does not vary uniformly in time and space." These studies do not contradict the proposal that stylistic attributes do change through time or that design variation between sites can be used to assign gross dates to sites. They do, however, suggest that significant errors can be made in dating sites on the basis of stylistic attribute frequencies if rates of change and the causes of differential rates of change are not known and/or are not constant. Information on the cause of stylistic variation is thus needed.

Second, there are also problems with the use of designs to measure interaction intensities between sites. A more detailed criticism can be made of this type of study for two reasons. First, ethnographic analyses of studies of stylistic variation through space are easier to carry out than ethnographic studies of variation through time and are thus more numerous. Second, archaeological studies of stylistic variation through space frequently have provided more precise quantification and statistical analyses of patterns of stylistic variation. As a result, problems with the use of stylistic variation to measure characteristics of prehistoric organization or interaction are easier to document. Both ethnographic and archaeological data that do not equate degrees of stylistic similarity or variation with interaction intensities will now be considered.

Ethnographic studies
A number of studies of stylistic variation in artifacts from modern preindustrial communities have been made since the initial proposals of a relationship between stylistic variation and organization and interaction. These studies include the research of Friedrich (1970), Stanislawski (1969, 1973), Stanislawski and Stanislawski (1974), Hodder (1977), and Longacre (1974, n.d.). While Longacre's fieldwork and analysis are still in progress, conclusions have been drawn from the other studies. On the basis of a study of Hopi ceramic production, the extent to which the diffusion of stylistic attributes is channeled by organizational units such as lineages, clans, or villages has been questioned (Stanislawski 1969, 1973; Stanislawski and Stanislawski 1974). The analysis indicated that among the Hopi, who occupy several villages on three mesas in northeastern Arizona, there are "mesawide styles, rather than tribal, village, or lineage or clan-owned designs" (Stanislawski and Stanislawski 1974:11). Friedrich's (1970) study of ceramic decoration in a Tarascan village in Mexico indicated that patterns of variation in some stylistic attributes but not in others were useful as indicators of interaction intensities between the potters. (The specific attributes will be discussed in Chapter 4.) In addition, her analysis suggested (1970:342) that "the success of any attempt to reconstruct interaction patterns depends upon the extent to which the artisans who produced the archaeological style were actually interested in the designs they painted." Finally, the study by Hodder (1977) included several types of objects

used by three tribal groups in western Kenya, and it is thus more comprehensive than Friedrich's or Stanislawski's analysis in regard to both the number of different groups and the variety of material items included. Hodder found that despite frequent interaction between individuals of different tribes, the distributions of many stylistic characteristics and material items primarily were confined to distinct tribal areas. He therefore concludes (1977:269) that "the distribution of material cultural traits . . . are not necessarily and wholly structured by patterns of interaction. It is quite possible to have distinct groups with distinct material cultures but who have very strong and frequent interaction." Thus, a number of ethnographic studies either have not supported or have suggested modifications in the use of stylistic similarities or variation to measure interaction intensities.

The results of these studies should not be accepted uncritically, however. In both the Hopi and Tarascan cases, for example, the context of pottery making is very different from many prehistoric situations. In both areas, ceramic vessels are produced to be sold in commercial markets, and there is evidence, at least for the Hopi (Bunzel 1972:83), that this trade has had important effects on the diffusion of designs from one potter to another. More importantly, none of these studies have provided quantified, objective measures of interaction intensities or of degrees of stylistic similarity. Thus, it is impossible to measure precisely the degree of relationship if any, between the variables.

Archaeological evidence
In addition to the ethnographic studies already discussed, a variety of archaeological evidence also does not support the use of degrees of stylistic similarity or variation to measure interaction intensities. First, if intersite design similarities do measure the intensity of interaction between communities, then the similarity between contemporaneous sites should decrease as distance between them increases. This relationship has been supported by studies of the movement of goods and people in industrialized societies (Olsson 1965; Zipf 1949), in contemporary nonindustrialized societies (Chisholm 1968; Hayano 1973; Kasakoff and Adams 1977), in historic groups (Deetz and Dethlefsen 1965) and in prehistoric societies (Ericson 1977; Hodder 1974; Pires-Ferreira 1973; Renfrew 1969; Sidrys 1977; Warren 1969). However, I have examined several sets of data on stylistic attribute distributions among prehistoric communities and have shown that in the majority of cases similarity between sites does not decrease with increasing distance between them (S. Plog 1976b). This relationship between distance and stylistic similarity also has been measured in some other recent studies. One of these analyses

also has shown no relationship between the variables (Fry and Cox 1974:221), while others have suggested a definite correlation (Engelbrecht 1979:5; Kay 1975:68; Washburn 1978:112–19; Washburn and Matson 1980).

In some of the latter cases, however, a statistical measure of the strength of the correlation suggests little relationship between the variables. For example, Washburn and Matson (1980) have suggested that one of their analyses revealed a close approximation between the geographical distance among a set of nine sites in the northwestern New Mexico area of the American Southwest and their stylistic distance as measured by their similarity in frequencies of ceramic design symmetry classes. They suggest (1980) that this was a result of groups interacting most intensively with adjacent populations. However, if a Pearson's correlation coefficient is calculated between the stylistic and geographical distances measured on the maps that they provide (Washburn and Matson 1980: Figures 3 and 6), the value of the coefficient is only 0.19 which is not statistically significant at the 0.05 level. Similarly, Washburn (1978:112–19) has argued that frequencies of ceramic design symmetry classes from the El Morro area of New Mexico are more similar to such frequencies in the nearby Upper Gila area than the more distant Salmon area, and this pattern is attributed to greater interaction between potters who live closer to each other (Kintigh 1979:59; Washburn 1978). However, Kintigh (1979:59) has noted that for two of Washburn's four symmetry indices the Salmon and Upper Gila areas are more similar to each other than to ceramics from the El Morro area despite the greater distance between the former areas.

An additional characteristic of those cases for which a relationship between geographic distance and stylistic similarities has been supported is that sites more distant than 30 to 40 kilometers are included. The relationship between the variables for sites located closer than such distances is not considered in these studies (e.g., Kay 1975) or does not appear to be strong (e.g., Engelbrecht 1979). However, many studies of actual interaction patterns (e.g., Olsson 1965) have shown decreases in interaction frequency over smaller distances, such as 5 kilometers or more. Thus, the proposed stylistic similarity–interaction relationship again is not supported.

A second problem with the stylistic similarity–interaction relationship is illustrated by a comparison between ceramic design similarities among prehistoric communities in a single valley, the Hay Hollow Valley in east-central Arizona, and design similarities among rooms within a single community, the Carter Ranch Site, in that valley. A discussion of these data is given in two papers by Longacre (1964a, 1970). It is clear from the following statements that those who have proposed the relationship between stylistic similarities and interaction intensities would expect that rooms within a single site would have more similar ceramic designs than would two separate communities.

> Closer bonds might be created through more intimate contact among the villages of a single valley . . . There may be more similarities in shared elements of design among the pottery of these villages when compared to the ceramics of other villages in neighboring valleys. Below this level of analysis would be the ceramics of the village. We may discover an accepted style of design common to a village within the broader sphere of the areal or "valley" tradition. If present, this village tradition would be based on intimate daily contact and would to some extent be kin-based [Longacre 1964a:28].

> Most archaeologists seem to agree that these style zones reflect learning: potters watched and copied the styles of nearby potters. There is more shared information within settlements than between settlements, within settlement clusters than between settlement clusters and so on [Martin and Plog 1973:259].

These statements should hold for contemporaneous communities if the proposed relationship between design similarities and interaction is true, but it certainly should hold when the comparison, as in this case, is between similarities among a set of noncontemporaneous sites [according to dates in Martin, Rinaldo, and Longacre (1960, 1961a, 1964)] and similarities among rooms in a pueblo in which there is "only a weak case for temporal differences causing sample variation" (Freeman and Brown 1964:140). Histograms of the design similarities among sites and among rooms are presented in Figure 1.1. The similarity measure is Pearson's r, and the coefficients were calculated using all 175 elements in Longacre's design classification (1970) and all sites in the Hay Hollow Valley for which design frequencies are given in Martin, Rinaldo, and Longacre (1964). The mean for each set of similarity coefficients is indicated by the vertical dotted line. The histograms show that contrary to expectations, design similarities among different sites are higher than similarities among rooms of a single site.

Finally, as noted, both a high level of intersite stylistic similarity and a low level of intrasite homogeneity have been considered to be indicative of high intensities of interaction between communities as a result of the increasing diffusion of designs between villages with increasing interaction such as the movement of women upon marriage (Connor 1968; Engelbrecht 1974; Leone 1968; Tuggle 1970; Whallon 1968). However, the two measures have not covaried in the

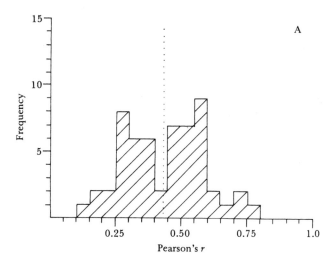

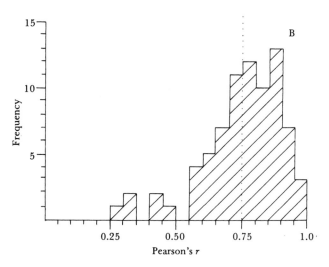

Figure 1.1. Histograms of similarity coefficients among rooms in the Carter Ranch Site (A) and sites in the Hay Hollow Valley (B).

expected manner. Whallon's (1968, 1969) studies of stylistic variation in twelfth century through fifteenth or sixteenth century ceramics from New York State showed that while the level of style homogeneity increased through time, intersite similarity also increased. In an additional study of sixteenth and seventeenth century ceramic designs from New York State, Engelbrecht (1974:57–9) found no patterned covariation between within site homogeneity and intersite similarity. Intersite similarity tended to increase while intrasite homogeneity did not consistently increase or decrease. In the American Southwest, Leone's (1968) and Connor's (1968) studies showed increasing village stylistic homogeneity at a period of time for which Tuggle (1970) found increasing intersite design similarity. Thus, the predicted relationship between intersite stylistic similarity and intrasite homogeneity has not been supported empirically.

Whallon (1969:15) has explained the covariation of intrasite homogeneity and intersite similarity in his data in the following way:

> As long as all communities share a common pool or repertoire of frequent and rare elements, which is maintained through communication or more strongly through the actual movement of women, an increase in . . . homogeneity will produce an intensification of the frequency or rarity of elements in the repertoire and thereby bring about a more or less automatic increase in similarity between sites.

However, this statement is not consistent with an earlier proposal by Whallon (1969:15).

> Increasing internal homogeneity of assemblages in terms of discrete stylistic elements may thus be seen as a result of the influence of [two] factors . . . which restrict, in a regional and within-community sense respectively, the range of variation to which a girl is exposed in the constant and regularly repetitive manner necessary for definitive habit-formation in the learning process.

If all communities initially share a common pool of stylistic elements, then why should decreased interaction among villages result in a decrease in "the range of variation to which a girl is exposed"? The first statement assumes that the range of variation is the same within all communities whereas the second assumes that it is not. Furthermore, if all communities share a common pool of frequent and rare stylistic elements, then they should be highly similar initially. Increased homogeneity should not increase this similarity.

In addition to the expected pattern of covariation between intrasite stylistic homogeneity and intersite similarity, another test implication of the proposition that stylistic variation is determined by interaction intensities is that as intrasite homogeneity changes, overall regional homogeneity should remain constant. The same number of design traditions should exist in the region, but as interaction between villages decreases, these design traditions diffuse less and become more restricted to individual villages. Also, as intrasite homogeneity increases in an area, it would be expected that the level of homogeneity would be more than the degree of homogeneity within the region as a whole. However, empirical studies have not supported these predictions. First, Braun's (1977) analysis of ceramic decorative variation during the Middle and Late Woodland periods in the midwestern United States demonstrated that intrasite and regional homogeneity varied directly over time. When intrasite homogeneity increased, for example, regional homogeneity also increased. Second, Connor's reanalysis (reported in Tuggle 1970:75–6) of the data used in her 1968 paper showed that the frequencies of design attributes for her three sites, all of which had high levels of homogeneity when analyzed separately, were no less homogeneous when combined. Thus, regional homogeneity was not lower than intrasite homogeneity as expected, even during a time period when intrasite homogeneity was increasing.

A variety of studies thus do not support the relationship that some have proposed between interaction intensities and stylistic similarity and variation. It should be noted that there are different kinds of interaction (intermarriage, simple communication, economic cooperation) and different levels at which interaction can be analyzed (within sets of communities or among regions). The assumption evaluated here is that the stylistic similarity between *a pair of sites* varies directly with the *total amount of interaction* among the individuals inhabiting the sites. Also, the evidence presented is primarily from analyses of intersite stylistic similarities. However, it should be emphasized that the analyses of intrasite style distributions such as Longacre's (1970) and Hill's (1970) also have been based on the assumption that stylistic similarities measure interaction intensities. The demonstration that the assumption is incorrect thus suggests that the conclusions of both intrasite and intersite analyses are erroneous. Moreover, a number of problems have been shown to exist with some of the intrasite analyses (S. Plog 1976a). These include the use of inappropriate statistical methods, such as Longacre's application of multiple regression analysis in his study of design distributions at the Carter Ranch Site, and the lack of demonstration of statistically significant spatial clusters of ceramic designs. My reanalysis (S. Plog 1976a) of some of the data on stylistic variation at the Carter Ranch Site and at Broken K Pueblo has questioned the reality of the clusters that have been proposed at each site.

Finally, other criticisms of the second type of stylistic analysis have been made. Allen and Richardson (1971) have agreed that archaeologists can discover "aggregates" and "demonstrate long range change in the composition of local aggregates," but without offering an alternative explanation, they have questioned the conclusion that the patterns isolated by Hill (1970) and Longacre (1970) indicated location of residence groups. Stanislawski (1973:120–1) and L. Johnson (1972) have proposed that the patterns may represent the location of "ad hoc" work groups of neighbors rather than residence groups. This explanation, however, also is based on the assumption that design similarities measure interaction intensities.

Conclusions

The discussion has identified problems that arise in interpreting stylistic attributes as primarily varying temporally or as primarily varying in response to patterns of social interaction. In order to learn what, if any, aspects of stylistic variation may be associated with social phenomena and what variables must be taken into consideration in using attribute frequencies to date sites, it is necessary to understand the causes of stylistic variation. However, a major weakness of past studies is that they have not attempted to determine these causes; time is a reference dimension rather than a causal variable. The proposal that interaction intensities explain stylistic variability always has been assumed and not demonstrated. Thus, a significant question that needs to be answered is what causes stylistic attributes to vary? In this study, I will attempt to provide some initial answers to this question.

While I feel that the results of the research described here are relevant to stylistic analyses in general, the reader should be aware that the research primarily evolved from my interest over the past few years in the use of stylistic similarities and stylistic variation in ceramics to measure prehistoric organizational and interaction patterns; weaknesses in that approach have already been noted (S. Plog 1976a, 1976b, 1978). Thus, this study is in part addressed to questions that were raised in my evaluation of that approach. In addition, because the emphasis in those studies is on stylistic variation in ceramics, particularly ceramic designs, the research described here also concentrates on ceramic design variation. Thus, the next chapter focuses on some possible explanations of that variation.

2

The hypotheses

In this chapter, I will discuss a series of hypotheses which may explain part, but not all, of ceramic design variation within or between sites. A basic premise that guided the formulation of these hypotheses is that design variation is a result of a number of different factors. That is, no one variable will explain a large percentage of the variation in design frequencies but, rather, there are multiple factors each of which will explain a portion of the variation. At a time when archaeologists have increasingly recognized the complex nature of cultural systems, it is surprising and unfortunate that many of those studying ceramic designs have assumed that design variation is not a complex phenomenon and thus could be described and explained very simply.

This oversimplification can be illustrated in several ways. First, there has been a highly selective use of ethnographic information. The primary ethnographic information that was emphasized by studies in the American Southwest, for example, was Bunzel's discovery that Pueblo potters of the 1920s primarily had learned ceramic designs from their mothers (Bunzel 1972:54). This information led to the proposal that design clusters within archaeological sites could be interpreted as the loci of matrilocal residence groups. However, other ethnographic data that would affect the probability that this proposal would be true were ignored (Stanislawski 1973). One example of this is the village specialization in ceramic production among the Hopi. If a village did not even manufacture its own pottery, spatial clusters of designs in a village will not indicate residence groups. While it has never been demonstrated that specialization in ceramic manufacture existed among *most* prehistoric Southwestern groups, it has never been demonstrated that it did not. Furthermore, for some groups such as late prehistoric pueblos in the Rio Grande Valley specialization has been demonstrated (Shepard 1942).

In addition to the selective use of ethnographic data relevant to the explanation of design variation, the correspondence between the systemic context of artifacts prehistorically and their archaeological context (Schiffer 1972) often has not been assessed. For example, there was evidence at Broken K that rooms were filled with trash (Hill 1970:30–1). Sherds from a single vessel were even found in rooms in different room blocks separated by a plaza (Martin, Longacre, and Hill 1967:136). Despite this evidence, Hill still used designs on ceramics in room fills in isolating the proposed residence groups. Also, it seems to have been assumed that artifacts from room floors were, in Schiffer's (1972) terms, de facto or primary refuse and could not be secondary refuse.

Oversimplification also has occurred in other ways. While relatively complex statistical procedures have been used in some instances, many of the basic assumptions and requirements of such procedures, such as necessary sample sizes or the degree of normality of the data sets, have been given little consideration (Baldwin 1975; Lischka 1975; S. Plog 1976a). The difficulty of developing meaningful design classification systems is an additional topic that has not been adequately discussed in some studies. This problem will be discussed in greater detail in Chapter 4.

It is reasonable and necessary in building models to control the effect of other variables by holding them constant or to simplify the models initially by ignoring some variables. At the same time, as these models are developed, applied, and tested, the effect of other factors must be gradually considered if the model is to be realistic. I submit that the model of the relationship between design variation and social organization that was originally constructed primarily by Deetz and Longacre was never developed past the initial stage in most of the research that followed. Except for a few changes in methods of data analysis, the studies of Gerald (1975), Hanson (1975), and Clemen (1976), for example, are duplicates of the previous studies done in the first half of the 1960s. The model was never developed to the point that it was realistic. Neither the complexity of cultural systems nor the complexity of understanding the processes accounting for the formation of the archaeological record were dealt with. Only recently have a few studies (Braun 1977, Conkey 1978, Rubertone 1978, Voss 1976) made significant improvements.

The hypotheses presented next represent an attempt to make our efforts to explain design variation more realistic. The effect of subsistence-settlement systems, ceramic exchange, temporal changes in design, and vessel shape on design variability will be considered. We can look at these hypotheses as an initial step in developing models to account for ceramic design variation.

Subsistence-settlement systems

One of the most important archaeological concepts developed in the 1950s and early 1960s was that of subsistence-settlement systems.

Human populations adapt not only to the immediate area of a community but also to regions. Because of the differential distribution of natural resources, different types of activities will be carried out in different parts of the regions. The cultural adaptations to this differential distribution in terms of exploitation strategies are enormously varied. Entire groups may move seasonally as resources become available in different areas, small groups may separate from larger groups at certain periods to exploit particular resources, resources rather than people may be moved between areas, or a number of other options may be chosen. As Binford (1964:432) has stated,

> It is a known and demonstrable fact that sociocultural systems vary in the degree to which social segments perform specialized tasks, as well as in the cyclical pattern of task performance at any given location. These differences have spatial correlates with regard to the loci of task performance; hence we expect sites to vary formally and spatially with regard to the nature of the tasks performed at each, and the social composition of the units performing the tasks.

One of the results of many adaptive strategies is that a single group of people, whether we are speaking of a nuclear family or a larger social group, may inhabit a number of sites in a single year and a large number of sites over a period of 25 or even 10 years. Thus, the artifacts manufactured by this group of people will be deposited on a number of sites. The magnitude of this artifact distribution is a result of two factors: (1) the amount of movement of individuals within a single year's cycle, and (2) the frequency with which sites (both limited activity and more permanent sites) are reoccupied from year to year. The greater the amount of movement within a single year's cycle and the lower the rate at which sites are reoccupied, the greater will be the spatial distribution of artifacts of a single group of people both in total area and in number of sites. Any study of the spatial distribution of stylistic attributes must take this into consideration. In attempting to measure interaction between communities by measuring the similarity of the pottery designs found at the communities, as many people have done, we could in fact be dealing with pottery from two communities which were both inhabited by the same group of people.

Stylistic analyses that have been carried out generally have not discussed this factor. It seems to have been assumed implicitly that the activities conducted by a group within a year's cycle were carried out at one site and that villages were inhabited for long periods of time, for it is difficult to find any statements in these studies refuting this tacit proposition. It is assumed implicitly in the studies concerning intersite relationships that the sites being dealt with were contemporaneous and occupied by different groups of people, despite the fact that the time periods or phases being considered were 80 (Pollnac and Rowlett 1977), 150 (Tuggle 1970), or 200 years (Longacre 1964a) long. As Gumerman (1970:28) has noted, "Too often archaeologists assume sites are contemporaneous because their ceramic assemblages are roughly similar . . . The question of contemporaneity has important consequences in such questions as population patterns and inter-site relationships."

Unfortunately, there has been little study of the lengths of site occupations. In the American Southwest, Schiffer's (1976) analysis of the tree-ring and radiocarbon dates from the Joint Site indicates that it was probably occupied between 33 and 58 years. Dean's (1970) study of the tree-ring dates from the sites of Betatakin and Kiet Siel suggest they were occupied for 33 and 50 to 60 years, respectively. Most occupation dates suggested for sites in the Southwest are longer than this, but they are usually based on pottery dates or radiocarbon dates, which are not as precise as tree-ring dates or are based on fewer tree-ring dates than were available to Schiffer and Dean. The Joint Site, Betatakin, and Kiet Siel are all large sites with 33, 135, and 155 pueblo rooms, respectively (Schiffer 1976:145; Dean 1970:158). If these sites were only occupied for 50 to 60 years, it is very possible that many of the smaller sites that make up a large majority of the prehistoric sites in the American Southwest were occupied for much shorter periods.

In some other areas of the world, short occupation spans for sites also have been suggested. For the area of New York State occupied historically by Iroquois groups, Engelbrecht (1974:54) has suggested that sites were abandoned by those groups every 8 to 20 years as a result of the practice of a swidden agricultural strategy and the exhaustion of firewood near the sites. Smith (1978:191–5) has argued that many Powers phase sites in southeastern Missouri were occupied for less than 5 years. In eastern Wisconsin, Overstreet (1978:40) estimates that during the period from A.D. 1000 to 1300, a time when the duration of site occupations had increased over previous periods, sites may have been abandoned every 3 to 15 years.

Thus, evidence indicates that in some areas the length of time that sites were occupied is considerably shorter than the duration of the temporal phases to which archaeologists assign them. In many cases, therefore, sites that date to the same phase are not likely to have been occupied contemporaneously. For example, if a pair of sites were each occupied for 20 years but only could be placed within a phase 100 years long, there would be a probability of less than 50 percent that the occupations of the sites overlapped in time. Yet, the degree of stylistic similarity between sites of the same phase has been used to estimate the intensity of interactions between the inhabitants of these sites. It does not make sense, however, to discuss the interaction between the population of two communities that were not even occupied at the same time.

The concept of subsistence-settlement systems is, then, an important concept to be considered when analyzing stylistic attributes. Adaptive strategies determine the frequency and type of movement throughout a region and thus determine the deposition of the artifacts made by a group of people. The subsistence-settlement system and its effect on artifact distribution must, therefore, be considered when attempting to explain the spatial variability in the distribution of stylistic attributes.

Vessel shape and use
Only a few ethnographic or archaeological studies have examined the relationship between vessel shape and design features. By "vessel shape" I mean not only different types of vessel forms such as bowls, jars, and pitchers, but also the parts of a single vessel that have different shapes such as the body and neck of a jar. In the studies that have been made, some interesting relationships have been found. Friedrich, in her study of pottery making in the Mexican village of San Jose, found that the decorated area of a jar was subdivided into areas such as the neck, shoulder, and bottom (1970:334–5). In analyzing the design configurations of the different spatial divisions, she noted that some configurations were found only in particular divisions. Friedrich (1970:335) argued that in part this could be explained by the fact that "the use of each configuration is determined by its shape and, therefore, in part by the shape of the spatial divisions." At the same time, Friedrich noted that the distribution of some configurations could not be explained in this way and she concluded that their use was simply restricted to certain areas (1970:335).

A similar pattern has been discovered in other ethnographic studies and in archaeological studies in a variety of areas. In her ethnographic study of pottery making at the pueblo of Zuni in the American Southwest, Bunzel notes that the neck and body areas of jars are decorated differently: "It is an important characteristic of Zuni decoration that all designs are born to a certain station in life. A neck design can never rise to the dignity of a stomach design, and no stomach design would demean itself to the extent of adorning a neck [1972:16]." This was not the case, however, at the Hopi villages or at Acoma where the exteriors of jars were treated as single fields (Bunzel 1972:20, 38). Different patterns of decoration on different areas of the same vessel also has been noted for potters in the Caribbean

(Rouse 1965:89), for some prehistoric time periods in the Ica Valley of Peru (Menzel 1976), on pottery from the modern village of Quinua in Peru (Arnold 1972), and for some prehistoric vessels from the Reserve (Barter 1957:116) and Mesa Verde (Rohn 1971:149) areas of the American Southwest.

Use of different designs on vessels of different shapes has been documented in several regions, also. Amsden (1936) found an association between design features and vessel shape in his study of Hohokam pottery from the prehistoric Southwest. Amsden (1936:5) distinguishes between bowls and plates that are open forms and jars that are closed forms, and he notes that jars must be decorated on their exterior surfaces and the interiors of bowls are usually decorated. These surfaces have a different character in that the body or shoulder area of a jar "is a rectangular band with a definite upper and lower limit while the inside of a bowl is a circular field with only an outer limit. Some designs fit both about equally well, but most do not" (Amsden 1936:16). Amsden's analysis supported this point, showing a correlation between vessel form and type of design pattern (1936:23). Bunzel (1972:42) notes that designs on Hopi bowls are not used on Hopi jars. She did not find this pattern at other pueblos. Other cases in which it has been noted that decorative patterns vary between different vessel forms include ethnographic studies of pottery from the Yucatecan Maya area of Mexico (Thompson 1958:145) and the village of Quinua in Peru (Arnold 1972:866–77; 1975:189) and analyses of archaeological collections from the Valdivia period (3000 to 1500 B.C.) in Ecuador, the Upper Gila (Washburn 1977:184 and Cibola (Redman 1978:181) areas of the American Southwest, and for several prehistoric periods in the Ica Valley of Peru (Menzel 1976; Menzel, Rowe, and Dawson 1964). In addition, Fry and Cox (1974) found different patterns of intersite stylistic similarity for two different vessel forms from the Tikal area of the Maya region.

This evidence thus suggests that the different decorative fields of a single vessel form and also different vessel forms may be painted with different designs. The choice of design attributes by potters often is contingent (Deetz 1968b:35) on the choice of vessel form. If in a given instance this relationship is true, it would affect the similarities of design features found at different sites or different areas within a site. If vessel form is related to vessel function, as will be argued next, and if different functions or different proportions of several functions are carried out at these spatial units (or sites), then different frequencies of vessel forms will be found at these units. The level of design similarity between units may thus be affected if different design features are associated with these different vessel forms. Primarily, bowls may be found at one site while jars may be predominate at another. As a result, the design features at the two sites may be less similar than two sites where bowls were the predominate form used. Intrasite variability could be affected also if different types of activities are carried out in different areas of the sites or in different types of rooms. Some studies that have attempted to infer organizational or interactional patterns from design variation, particularly some of those conducted using ceramics from the eastern or midwestern United States, have controlled this problem by analyzing only certain vessel forms or particular areas of a vessel, or by carrying out separate analyses of design frequencies on different areas of a vessel or different vessel forms (e.g., Braun 1977; Deetz 1965; Engelbrecht 1974; S. Plog 1976b).

Research in progress on stylistic variation on early Neolithic ceramics from northern Europe (Voss 1976) and on engraved bone and antler from Cantabrian Spain (Conkey 1978) also is attempting to control or measure the effect of artifact shape on decorative variation. However, this problem has received little attention in other design-interaction studies, particularly those done using ceramics from the southwestern United States. That is, design frequencies on different vessel forms and different areas of a vessel have not been analyzed separately. There also have been few, if any, explicit studies in design analyses in general of the degree to which design differences between vessel forms or areas of vessels can account for the degree of ceramic design variation within a site or between sites, although this question has been considered in at least one study of stylistic variation on other artifacts. Close (1978) compared stylistic characteristics on four functional classes of backed bladelets from North Africa and found no significant differences between the classes. However, given the data on ceramic design patterns just discussed, the importance of this factor should be tested when we attempt to explain intersite or intrasite variation in ceramic designs.

Exchange
The topic of material exchanges between prehistoric groups is a topic that has recently begun to receive a considerable amount of attention in most areas (Earle and Ericson 1977; Sabloff and Lamberg-Karlovsky 1975) including the American Southwest (DeGarmo 1977; Hudson 1975; Jack 1971; Warren 1969; Weigand, Harbottle, and Sayre 1977). At least in part, this renewed interest in exchange has been the result of an increased desire to measure the interaction between populations. It is this same desire that has resulted in the studies of intersite stylistic similarities and differences.

The knowledge that ceramics were exchanged in large quantities in some areas was gained through detailed petrographic studies such as Shepard's (1942, 1948) in the 1930s and 1940s. However, the cases in which exchange has been demonstrated often have been assumed to be isolated examples. In very few studies dealing with sites or regions in the American Southwest, for example, will we find statements suggesting that a large percentage of the ceramics from the sites or regions were imported or exported. Neither will we often find that any method such as petrographic analysis was used to analyze the ceramics to test this possibility. This assumption that ceramic exchange was not frequent seems to have resulted from an assumption about the causes of exchange in general prehistorically. This assumption is that trade occurs only when a group lacks a critical raw material. Inasmuch as the raw materials, such as clay, required for ceramic production are available in most areas, it has been assumed that ceramic exchange was not necessary.

Several other factors could, however, result in the exchange of pottery despite the widespread abundance of raw materials. First, while the raw materials for ceramic production may be available in a number of areas, not all such materials are of equal quality (Arnold 1975:192; Windes 1977:294–5). Arnold (1975) has discussed an eth-nographic case in which the quality of ceramic raw materials appears to have been one factor leading to specialization in ceramic produc-tion in the area. Second, in the instances in which ceramic exchange has been demonstrated, it has sometimes been argued that the ce-ramic vessels were only containers used to transport resources that were differentially distributed so that some groups did not have access to them (Windes 1977:293–4) or resources such as food which were in short supply. It is possible that ceramic vessels were traded in this manner, as ethnographic examples are known (Russell 1975:124). However, there is no good prehistoric evidence that sup-ports or disproves these hypotheses.

In addition to these possible reasons for ceramic exchange, two additional hypotheses can be offered. First, even if economic necessi-ties are the prime factors leading to the exchange of goods, products that are not economic necessities may have an important functional role in the exchange system (Rappaport 1968:105–9). Rappaport (1968:106) has suggested that in a system where exchange is directly between individuals, the system would not be viable if only critical subsistence items were traded because of inequities in production. He hypothesizes that this may be true primarily in linear as opposed to "weblike" networks (1968:107). In these linear systems where produc-ing groups may be separated by several intervening groups, formal trading arrangements such as trade partners would not be sufficient to induce the necessary exchange. As a result, insufficiencies would develop because the production of the commodities supplied by one village "would not be determined by the demand for that commodity, but by the demand for the commodity for which it was exchanged"

(Rappaport 1968:106). Rappaport suggests that the inclusion in the exchange system of nonutilitarian goods along with utilitarian items might stimulate production and aid the movement of utilitarian goods. The demand for nonutilitarian goods needed for bride-price or some other nonsubsistence purpose might be unlimited, particularly if the nonutilitarian goods are perishable (1968:108). There would thus be a continual production of the utilitarian items for the purpose of exchange for nonutilitarian goods and the distribution of utilitarian goods would be aided. A simulation model has been used to test the plausibility of Rappaport's proposal and has indicated that the movement of nonutilitarian items possibly could function to regulate exchange systems (Wright and Zeder 1977).

While ceramic vessels in most areas would be classified as utilitarian goods, they may have been inessential in areas where the resources required for pottery manufacture were available everywhere. It is, therefore, possible to suggest, but in no way demonstrate, that prehistorically pottery could have been an item that was exchanged for the purpose of aiding the distribution of essential utilitarian goods.

The possible causes for ceramic trade discussed are all ultimately a result of the necessity of exchange caused by the differential distribution of natural resources. However, ethnographic evidence indicates that trade also may be the result of artificial differences in the production of craft goods that cannot be explained in terms of the distribution of resources in the environment (Chagnon 1968; R. I. Ford 1972a; Specht 1974; Voorhies 1973). These artificial differences are thus culturally imposed rather than determined by the physical environment. As the discussion of Sahlins (1972), Chagnon (1968), and R. I. Ford (1972a) indicate, exchange systems are important in adapting to a group's social environment as well as to its physical environment. These artificial differences among groups in the production of craft goods thus may be the result of the social importance of trade. An example of this is Chagnon's description of exchange among the Yanamamo. Chagnon (1968:10) notes that each Yanamamo village produces one or more special products but that this specialization cannot be explained by the distribution of necessary raw materials. Each village is capable of being self-sufficient. He argues that trade is an important factor in alliance formation and provides the following example to support his proposal.

> Clay pots are a good example of the specialization in labor that characterizes Yanamamo production and trade. The Momaribowei-teri . . . are allied to both Koabawa's group and the people of a distant Shamatari village, the latter being mortal enemies of Koabawa. When I first began fieldwork, I visited Momaribowei-teri, specifically asking

them if they knew how to make clay pots. They all vigor-
ously denied knowledge of pot-making, explaining that
they once knew how to make them but had long since
forgotten. They explained that their allies, the Mowarao-
aba-teri, made them in quantities and provided all they
needed, and therefore they did not have to make them
anymore. They also added that the clay in the area of
their village was not of the proper type for making pots.
Later in the year their alliance with the pot maker grew
cool because of a war, and their source of pots was shut
off. At the same time, Koabawa's group began asking
them for clay pots. The Momaribowei-teri promptly re-
sponded by "remembering" how pots were made and
"discovering" that the clay in their neighborhood was in-
deed suitable for pot manufacturing. They had merely
created a local shortage of the item in order to rely on an
ally for it, giving sufficient cause to visit them [Chagnon
1968:100–1].

Thus, because of the social importance of trade we might expect
exchange in craft goods prehistorically despite the uniform distribution of the necessary raw materials.

The frequency of ceramic exchange in most areas is unknown
because of the lack of attention the subject has received. While it has
been assumed that ceramic exchange was not a frequent occurrence,
the previous discussion has shown why the reasoning behind this
assumption may be incorrect. In addition, in a variety of regions an
increasing number of studies of the chemical composition (Bennyhoff and Heizer 1965; Deutchman 1979; Hall 1971; Harbottle and
Sayre 1975; Irwin 1978a, 1978b; Perlman and Asaro 1971; Sayre
and Chan 1971) and mineralogical composition (Bareis and Porter
1965; Warren 1969) of ceramics, and of technological or stylistic
attributes (Fry and Cox 1974; G. A. Johnson 1973; Lathrap 1973)
have suggested the exchange of ceramic vessels prehistorically; the
lack of comparable studies in most areas of the world makes the
frequent assumption of infrequent trade a dangerous one. The
studies cited suggest that ceramic exchange may have been a frequent occurrence prehistorically. If it was, spatial variability in the
distribution of ceramic designs may be explained by the spatial distribution of trade networks.

Temporal variability
As noted, studies of design variability through time were the primary
type of design analyses during the period between 1920 and 1960.
For example, even Cronin's (1962) study of decorative variation in
one area of the American Southwest, which is often cited by those

using design similarities to measure social interaction, was primarily concerned with the relationship of designs on pottery types through time. The primary conclusion reached in these early design studies, that ceramic designs changed through time, basically has been ignored in the more recent studies that have focused on the relationship between stylistic variation and social relationships. I feel that this was in part a result of the often repeated statement that time is only a reference dimension and not an explanatory variable. Since temporal variation could not be used as an alternative explanation of the patterns isolated in some recent studies, it was not considered.

However, temporal variation cannot be ignored in these types of studies even if time is not an explanatory variable. If design similarities and differences between spatial units can be shown to correlate with temporal differences in the occupation of these units, then synchronic explanations of the similarities and differences, such as the proposal that they are a result of different intensities of interaction between the populations of the units, are not likely to be valid. If our explanation of variability in the similarity of rooms or sites through space are synchronic ones, we must make sure that the data being analyzed are synchronic. Design studies that attempt synchronic explanations must, therefore, control the dimension of time.

An important topic which must be considered in order to control the temporal dimension is the rate and pattern of design change through time. In most recent studies, it has been implicitly assumed that design change was not continuous through time but rather there was relative stability in designs for a period of time, then rapid change, then stability, and so on, as Spaulding (in Willey and Phillips 1958:15) has argued. This is shown by the frequent use of pottery types, defined by types of designs, to date sites used in these studies and to assign them to temporal phases. When sites of the same phase are analyzed, however, design similarities and differences are explained not by design change through time but design *diffusion* as a result of interaction intensities between sites. This approach assumes that the designs defining pottery types suddenly appear and disappear. Martin and Plog (1973:256-7) have suggested, however, that rates of increase and decrease in the abundance of pottery types vary considerably. Their analysis of Breternitz's tree-ring dates for pottery types in the American Southwest suggested that "different pottery types are adopted at different rates by different populations who are adapting to different environmental conditions" (1973:256). In addition, studies of stylistic change during historic (Deetz and Dethlefsen 1965, 1967; Dethlefsen and Deetz 1966) and recent time periods (Kroeber 1919) have shown that stylistic change is continuous and that rates of change vary.

Studies of rates of prehistoric design change are thus needed.

Earlier design studies have indicated that designs can change greatly within a period of 100 years. For example, many of the pottery types defined for the American Southwest have estimated durations of only 100 years or less (H. S. Colton 1955). Studies have also shown that the degree of design similarity between sites whose average occupation dates (the median of their phase dates) differ by 150 to 200 years is correlated with the differences in the occupation dates (Tuggle 1970; S. Plog 1976a).

We do not have, however, measures of the rate of design change within phases, within periods of 25 to 75 years. Will the rate of change be continuous and at a high enough rate so that the degree of design similarity among sites whose occupations are separated by 25 to 75 years will be highly correlated with the temporal difference in their occupations? If a high correlation is found, then in order to study synchronic design variation it would be necessary to demonstrate that the sites being analyzed were contemporaneous. To demonstrate contemporaneity during such a short time period would require precise temporal control such as tree-ring dates for each site. Not only would the sites have to be occupied contemporaneously but also their length of occupation would have to be similar. If designs are changing continuously, then a site occupied for 25 years would have less design variation than a site occupied for 50 years (Englebrecht 1971:18). The question of the rate of design change is thus an important one that needs to be answered.

Explanation and nonexplanation
Four factors, subsistence-settlement systems, vessel shape, ceramic exchange, and temporal changes in design have been proposed as possible explanations of ceramic design variability. It could be argued that these factors are not true explanatory variables. For example, trade, like diffusion, is often considered to be an event that requires explanation rather than treatment as an explanatory variable. However, in discussing whether these factors are or are not explanatory variables, it is important to delineate the questions being asked. One of the questions that has been asked by some researchers is simply *why designs vary*. That is, why are the designs painted by one potter similar or different from those painted by another potter? The variables already discussed will not explain variation in the designs painted by different potters. They are, however, explanatory variables when it is the variation in design frequencies within or between sites that we are trying to understand. Explaining variation among potters and explaining variation among spatial units are both important; they are also interrelated problems. If we know why the designs painted by different potters vary, it will usually help explain why design frequencies vary within or between sites. At the same

time, it will have little value if, as argued previously, a large percentage of the ceramics found at a group of sites were made at an unknown number of communities 50 miles away by an unknown number of potters, or if we cannot be sure that the ceramics made at two different sites were not made by the same person. Whether we call the factors discussed here "control" variables, as some people would, or explanatory variables is irrelevant. The variables will not explain why the designs painted by two potters are similar or different, but they may help archaeologists understand intrasite and intersite variation in ceramic designs. The importance of answering this question has already been demonstrated.

3

The data base and data collection

The utility of the hypotheses presented will be assessed by evaluating their importance in explaining design variation in one area of the American Southwest. The particular region to be considered is the southern part of the Chevelon Creek drainage in east-central Arizona and the Phoenix Park, Day, and Cottonwood Wash drainages to the east of Chevelon Creek. Inasmuch as these areas have only recently received the attention of archaeologists and little published material is available, I will summarize the work that has been done in the area and the knowledge of the area's prehistory. First, however, a brief outline of the prehistory of the northern part of the American Southwest will be included for those who are unfamiliar with the area.

The American Southwest
The Chevelon Canyon area generally is considered part of the northern half of the American Southwest in terms of prehistoric cultural traits and evolutionary patterns. For the purpose of this study, the latter area is defined roughly as the northeastern and east-central parts of Arizona, the western half of New Mexico, the extreme southwestern portion of Colorado, and the southeastern corner of Utah. Several cultural units or areas have been defined within that general area, of which the most inclusive for the period after A.D. 1 are the Mogollon and Anasazi. These two units are distinguished on the basis of a number of stylistic characteristics such as extended versus flexed burials; brown versus gray colored plain ware pottery; Cibola versus Tusayan, Little Colorado, and Mesa Verde White Ware ceramics; and three-quarter versus full grooved axes. Mogollon stylistic characteristics primarily are found in the mountainous areas of east-central Arizona and west-central and southwestern New Mexico, whereas Anasazi stylistic characteristics are found through most of the remaining part of the northern Southwest. As noted, it is in the mountainous area of east-central Arizona that the Chevelon Canyon region is found.

While two different culture areas or traditions have been identified for the northern Southwest, similar evolutionary trajectories characterize both areas after A.D. 1 (Martin and Rinaldo 1951, Martin and Plog 1973). During the first five to six centuries after A.D. 1, a mixed subsistence strategy was practiced, including gathering wild plants, hunting, and the cultivation of corn, squash and probably beans by at least the end of the period. Populations likely moved throughout the year to exploit resources in different areas. Population density was probably very low and comparable to hunting and gathering populations in other arid areas of the world. Dwellings in most areas were pithouses or jacal (wattle-and-daub) structures built over shallow basins. The number of such structures on a site generally was low, suggesting that the populations inhabiting individual sites were small in number. For example, using data from several areas of the northern Southwest, F. Plog and others (1978:141) found an average of 1.3 structures per site prior to A.D. 800. However, some sites with as many as 20 to 30 structures are known from that period.

In many areas, population levels began to increase rapidly by A.D. 700 to 900 (F. Plog 1974, Gumerman 1975, Swedlund and Sessions 1976, Reher 1977), and several changes occurred in different aspects of the adaptive systems. As a result of the population increases, the mobility of populations and the size of the area they exploited probably decreased, a trend that will be discussed in more detail in the last chapter of this study. It has been suggested (Martin and Plog 1973:277, F. Plog 1974:42, Karlstrom and others 1976:154) that the dependence of populations on agriculture increased through time relative to the gathering of wild plants. Some recent studies (Stiger 1977) support this latter argument, while other analyses (Gasser n.d.) suggest fluctuations over time in the contribution of cultigens to the diet. Along with the hypothesized subsistence changes, it appears that sedentary populations had evolved by at least A.D. 700 to 900. This is suggested by the increase during that period in the amount of artifactual material deposited on sites as well as by increases in the frequency of storage rooms and/or pits. Also, in most areas a change to above-ground masonry habitation units occurs about A.D. 700 to 900. The average number of rooms on sites increases to 2.9 during the period from A.D. 800 to 1100 (F. Plog et al. 1978:141).

Through time, population levels continued to increase in most areas until either A.D. 1075 to 1125 or A.D. 1200 to 1275. Individual site size remained relatively constant in some of these areas, while sharp increases occurred in other regions with towns where fifty to several hundred habitation rooms developed. The average number of rooms per site increases to 9.5 (F. Plog and others

1978:141). Following this period of population increase, population levels dropped rapidly in almost all areas. Most regions were abandoned completely during one or two periods: (1) A.D. 1100 to 1150 or (2) A.D. 1250 to 1300. These abandonments have been attributed to a variety of different causes including climatic change, warfare, and populations exceeding the carrying capacity of their area.

The Chevelon drainage

The drainage of Chevelon Creek is an area of approximately 2070 square kilometers (800 square miles) forming a triangle with its northern point near Winslow, Arizona, and its base along the Mogollon Rim, as shown in Figure 3.1. There is a steady increase in elevation as we proceed from north to south, with the elevation at the confluence of Chevelon Creek and the Little Colorado River 1494 meters (4900 feet) and the elevation along the Mogollon Rim ranging from 2134 to 2286 meters (7000 to 7500 feet). There are also gradual changes in vegetation and rainfall from north to south. Vegetation varies from desert grassland at the northern edge of the drainage through juniper-pinyon woodland to a ponderosa pine forest at the southern edge. Annual rainfall increases from approximately 188 millimeters (7.4 inches) at Winslow at the extreme northern part of the area to 462 millimeters (18.2 inches) at the Chevelon Ranger Station in the extreme south. Soils are limestone derived along with a variety of sandy loams.

Previous data collection

The only archaeological research done in the area other than Fewkes' (1904) excavations at Chevelon Ruin at the northern limit of the drainage has been done by Wilson (1969), the Arizona State Museum (Vivian 1969) and by the Chevelon Archaeological Research Project (CARP) (F. Plog 1974, 1978). Wilson did limited survey work in the McDonald Canyon area northeast of the Chevelon drainage; in the Clear Creek, Chavez Pass, and Canyon Diablo areas to the west; around Meteor Crater to the north; and around the town of Heber within the drainage. However, the vast majority of archaeological research has been by CARP. In 1971, the project surveyed a stratified random sample of the drainage, covering approximately 1 percent of the area and discovering 348 sites. In 1972, 1973, and 1974, the project concentrated survey and excavation efforts in a 65-square kilometer (25-square mile) area bounded by Purcell Wash and Larson Draw in the southern part of the drainage. This area is shown in Figures 3.1 and 3.2. Both a systematic random sample of transects and block surveys were done in this area. Also, sample excavations have been undertaken at approximately twenty-four sites in that area. It is the ceramic material from sites within the

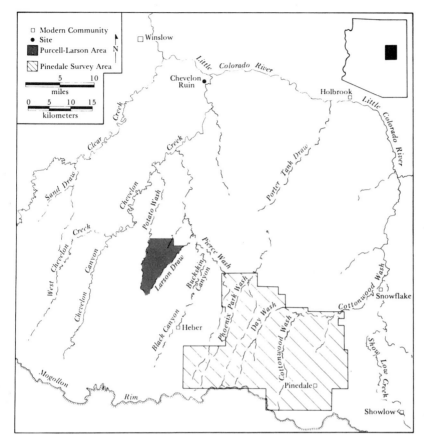

Figure 3.1. Locations in Arizona of the Purcell–Larson area and the Pinedale Survey area.

Purcell–Larson area that will provide the bulk of the data to be used in this study.

Culture history
In terms of the traditional definitions of the Southwestern culture areas discussed, the Chevelon drainage area would most appropriately be considered Mogollon, with the possible exceptions of some early (A.D. 600 to 800) sites in the extreme northern part that should be called Anasazi. The assignment of the drainage area as a whole to Mogollon is based on the types of corrugated and plain ware pottery. The painted ceramics found in the drainage area throughout the occupation there vary from Tusayan White Wares in the earliest periods to Little Colorado White Wares in the middle periods and then to Cibola White Wares in the last periods. Through-

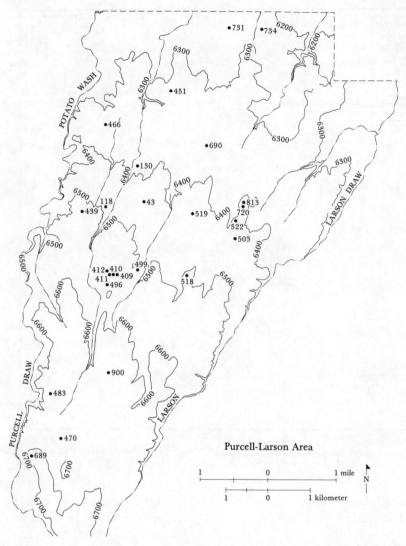

Figure 3.2. The Purcell–Larson area showing locations of sites discussed in the text.

out the entire time of occupation, however, the predominant plain and corrugated types are the red colored Mogollon Brown Ware as opposed to the gray colored types of the Tusayan Gray Ware series.

In architecture, the area is distinct in later time periods (A.D. 1100 to 1300) from what is considered characteristic of any prehistoric culture of the Southwest. While the primary habitation structures in the early periods are pithouses, which are found in most areas of the Southwest, in the later time periods the typical structure is horseshoe

Table 3.1. *Average number of rooms per square kilometer per 75-year interval within several time periods in the Chevelon and Hay Hollow areas*

Time period (A.D.)	Chevelon	Hay Hollow Valley
500–850	0.3	2.3
850–1050	2.3	2.7
1050–1125	1.9	3.5
1125–1200	5.0	8.5
1200–1275	9.3	3.1

shaped or three walled with boulder wall footings and a jacal super-structure. The open end of the horseshoe is always to the east. Excavation has indicated that this end is sometimes, but not always, closed by a jacal wall without a boulder footing. The observed sample of this type of structure is large because there has been little soil deposition in the area since the 1100s. As a result, the boulder footings are still visible and at some sites still stand 50 centimeters above the modern surface.

Although the density of such sites in parts of the Chevelon drainage is high, the size of sites as measured by the number of structures is very small. F. Plog (1972, 1974) has noted that the average number of rooms per site for the drainage as a whole is three, and within the Purcell–Larson area the average number of rooms varies from two to three during time segments within the period from A.D. 1050 to 1275. This area is thus very different from some areas of the Southwest in this regard. This difference in site size is particularly true in the later periods when the population agglomeration that occurs in many areas of the Southwest simply does not occur in Chevelon. The population figures in Table 3.1 that are constructed from figures given in F. Plog (1974) suggest, however, that population growth was occurring and continued when surrounding areas, such as the Hay Hollow Valley, were declining in population.

Settlement distribution

Site density in the drainage is highest in the juniper-pinyon woodland and lowest in the ponderosa pine forest. This is true in terms of both the total number of all sites and the total number of sites with structures. On the basis of the 1971 survey, the density of all sites and the density of sites with structures were estimated to be 10.8 sites and 1.3 sites per square kilometer, respectively, in the grassland and 28.1 sites and 6.8 sites per square kilometer, respectively, in the juniper-pinyon forest (F. Plog 1972). Sites were found in the ponderosa pine forest only along the canyon bottom, so the density in that vegetation zone is extremely low. The statistics indicate that the grassland zone had a higher proportion of sites without structures than did the juniper-pinyon zone. A large percentage of these grassland sites without structures had exclusively lithic artifacts (F. Plog 1972:5).

Within the juniper-pinyon forest, population density appears to increase as we proceed from north to south. The 1972 systematic random sample of the Purcell–Larson area provided estimates of 13.9 total sites and 6.4 sites with structures per square kilometer in the north where the elevation averages approximately 1890 meters (6200 feet) and the arboreal vegetation is 65 percent juniper (Acker 1973:6). In the south, where the elevation averages approximately 2042 meters (6700 feet) and 52 percent of all arboreal vegetation is pinyon, there are an estimated 24.3 total sites per square kilometer and 11.7 sites with structures per square kilometer (Acker 1973:6). Total annual rainfall also increases from north to south, and soil pH decreases. Acker's (1973) analysis of site density in the Purcell–Larson area has shown that it is directly correlated with the percentage of trees that are pinyon and with rainfall and inversely correlated with soil pH.

The dating scheme
Inasmuch as the ceramic dating of Chevelon sites is not typical of the Southwest, it will be described briefly. Ceramic classes were defined for black-on-white pottery on the basis of three attributes: (1) type of surface finish, polished (P) or slipped (S); (2) type of paint, mineral (M) or organic (O); and (3) type of temper, sherd (Sh), gray (G), or sand (S). "Gray" temper is actually a sherd temper also but looks very different macroscopically and microscopically from the category labeled "sherd" temper. Combinations of these three attributes logically define twelve classes, but sorting of thousands of black-on-white sherds on the basis of these attributes has shown that only three of them have frequencies greater than 5 percent at any site. These three combinations are; (1) polished surface, sand temper, organic paint (PSO); (2) slipped surface, sherd temper, organic paint (SShO); and (3) polished surface, gray temper, mineral paint (PGM). These three classes in the Chevelon classification are basically equivalent to the three primary white wares, Tusayan, Little Colorado, and Cibola White Wares, in the traditional Southwestern ceramic classification. The sorting of the Chevelon ceramics has, then, retested the discreteness of the traditional wares in the Southwest.

The Chevelon dating system is based on a seriation of the three primary Chevelon ceramic classes. The statistical aspects of the seriation are described by Read (1974). (However, the variable labels in Read's description [1974:Table 2] are in error. The labels for variables one and three should be reversed.) The most frequent early black-on-white class in Chevelon is PSO. As the frequency of PSO

Table 3.2. *Relative proportions of PGM, SShO, and PSO for the seven ceramic clusters isolated by Read (1974). (Period A is the latest and period G is the earliest temporal period)*

Period	Percentage PGM	Percentage SShO	Percentage PSO
A	82.3	4.2	3.0
B	50.6	21.5	12.2
C	40.6	48.0	3.4
D	7.2	81.0	4.7
E	28.1	4.7	51.0
F	5.3	32.7	51.4
G	10.2	14.4	25.0

PGM = Polished surface, gray temper, mineral paint.
SShO = Slipped surface, sherd temper, organic paint.
PSO = Polished surface, sand temper, organic paint.

decreases through time, SShO increases in relative frequency until it is the predominant black-on-white class. Finally, the most abundant late black-on-white class is PGM which increases as the frequency of SShO decreases. Seven temporal periods were defined by Read using the proportions of these three classes as raw data. The frequencies of the different classes in each of these periods are shown in Table 3.2.

The method of ceramic dating used in Chevelon by CARP is different from methods used in other areas of the Southwest because it is based on technological aspects of production rather than on types of ceramic designs. The dating system also implies that the ceramic history of the Chevelon drainage is different from other areas of the Southwest in that three different black-on-white wares are the most abundant wares at different points in time. In most areas of the Southwest, a single black-on-white ware is predominant throughout the occupation of the area. Given these distinct differences, we can ask what independent evidence exists to confirm the Chevelon ceramic dating. First, it can be noted that Wilson (1969:297) has found a similar sequence in regard to the relative frequencies of PSO and SShO through time in the areas surrounding the Chevelon drainage. He established this sequence using traditional southwestern types and wares, not by the attribute method used in Chevelon. Wilson states that "the post-A.D. 1100 decline in Tusayan White Ware and rise to favor of Little Colorado White Ware seems to hold true from one end of the survey area to the other" (1969:301). Furthermore, he notes that Snowflake Black-on-white, which is a Cibola White Ware and is thus equivalent to PGM, "appears to be a group 5 and 6 type within the survey area" (1969:312). His dates for groups 5 and

Table 3.3. *Proportions of PGM, SShO, and PSO and the range of outside tree-ring dates for Chevelon sites (CS)*

Site number	Range of outside dates	Percentage PGM	Percentage SShO	Percentage PSO	Sample size
470	1092	23	48	29	141
689	1160–1282	51	33	16	112
412	1195	78	21	1	471
690	1198	63	37	0	211
734	1191–1224	82	16	3	102
900	1239	90	9	1	343
43	1219–1240	87	12	2	611
731	1274	91	8	1	100
503	1281	78	22	0	1737

6 are A.D. 1100 to 1300 (1969:Table 2). Although this latter statement neither supports or negates the placement in the Chevelon ceramic dating of PGM as a class later than SShO, it does support the dating of PGM as later than PSO.

The Chevelon ceramic dating is also supported by the available tree-ring dates from Chevelon sites. The range of dates for the outside rings on beams from each site and the percentages of PSO, SShO, and PGM are shown in Table 3.3. It should be emphasized that none of these dates is a cutting date, that is, a beam with the bark present or with other evidence that the last ring that grew on the tree is still present. Only when such evidence is found can we be sure when the tree died or was cut down for the construction of the room. However, as will be considered next, it is probable that the latest date obtained for each site is close to the construction date for the sites. It also should be noted that the spatial distribution of the black-on-white ceramics from Chevelon site (CS) 503 suggests that it is a multicomponent site and that the tree-ring dates and building sequence at CS 689 suggest it was also multicomponent. The ceramic percentages for the tree-ring dated sites indicate that PGM does increase through time as SShO decreases.

Additional data collection
In order to test the hypotheses previously outlined, it was necessary to collect additional data to supplement that collected by CARP from 1971 to 1973. The additional data are of three types: (1) survey data and ceramic collections from the area to the east and southeast of the Purcell–Larson area, (2) intensive surface collections of sites within the Purcell–Larson area and within the new survey area, and (3) tree-ring dates from a larger number of Purcell–Larson sites than had been dated in this manner previously. The reasons for

collecting this data and the collection strategy and techniques will now be discussed.

Survey

Archaeological survey was conducted in the area shown in Figure 3.1 (which is east of the town of Heber) for one primary reason. It was considered possible that the many small sites in the Purcell–Larson area might be seasonal farming villages used primarily for agricultural activities during the summer. If they were seasonally occupied, the location of the more permanent habitation sites occupied during the remainder of the year was not known. Surveys to the west and north of the Purcell–Larson area by CARP and by Wilson (1969) had indicated that the types of sites in these areas were the same as the types in the Purcell–Larson area. The population density in these areas was also low during the peak population period in the Purcell–Larson area, a pattern that is not consistent with the hypothesis that populations seasonally moved from these areas to the Purcell–Larson area. Survey to the south of the Purcell–Larson area had indicated a low density of sites similar in size to those found in the Purcell–Larson area. Thus, the area east and southeast of the Purcell–Larson area seemed to be the only possible location of sites that might be more permanently occupied by populations constructing seasonal farming villages in the Purcell–Larson area. In addition, the little archaeological research that had been done near this area (Haury and Hargrave 1931) indicated the existence of at least a few large pueblo sites, such as Pinedale Ruin, which were occupied at approximately the same time as the period of highest population density in the Purcell–Larson area. For these reasons, it was decided to survey in the area just east and southeast of Purcell–Larson. Survey data would allow us to determine whether or not population density and site size in the area was comparable to Purcell–Larson and whether artifactual assemblages found on sites were different from those on Purcell–Larson sites, as would be expected if the latter sites were seasonally occupied by populations from the Pinedale area.

The survey strategy in the Pinedale area was threefold and is shown in Figure 3.3. First, a stratified random sample of transects was surveyed throughout the area. The transects were 1.6 to 2.3 kilometers long and 50 to 100 meters wide. Transects were chosen as the sampling unit because it has been shown that statistically, transects are one of the most efficient types of sampling units for estimating population densities (S. Plog 1976c). In addition, it has been shown that transects should theoretically result in the discovery of a greater number of sites, and experiments have verified this expectation (Plog, Plog and Wait 1978:398–402).

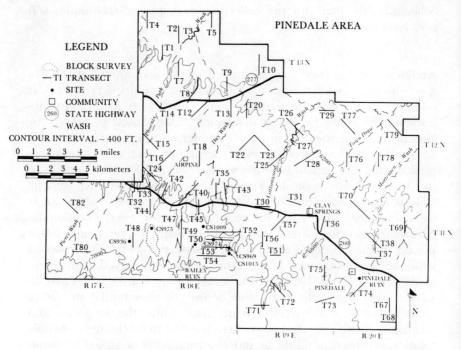

Figure 3.3. The Pinedale Survey area showing locations of transect and block surveys and locations of sites discussed in the text.

Initial stratification of the survey area was by range and township boundaries. Within each of the range and townships of the main survey area (T. 13 N., R. 18 E.; T. 12 N., R. 18 E.; T. 11 N., R. 18 E.; T. 12 N., R. 19 E.; T. 11 N., R. 19 E.) an average of seven randomly chosen transects (and a range of six to eight) were surveyed. Within each range and township, the section in which the transect was located was also chosen using a stratified random sample. It should be noted that the high density of transects in the northern sections of T. 11 N., R. 18 E. and T. 11 N., R. 19 E. was not a result of the randomness of the selection process. Dryness and the high probability of forest fires during the summer of 1974 prompted the U.S. Forest Service initially to prohibit us from surveying south of Arizona highway number 260. Because initial samples in the areas north of the two ranges and townships indicated had not shown a high density of sites, and because discussions with amateurs in the area and forest service personnel had indicated that the density of sites would increase as we surveyed farther south, we chose several random transects along the southern boundary of the area where we were allowed to survey. The southernmost areas were the northern sections of T. 11 N., R. 18 E. and T. 11 N., R. 19 E., which lay just north of highway 260. After those transects had been surveyed, the Forest Service allowed us access to the area south of Arizona highway number 260.

Stratified random transects were also chosen in the areas surrounding the main survey zone except in those areas which were: (1) outside the national forest and thus privately owned, (2) south of the Mogollon Rim and thus on the Fort Apache Indian Reservation where we did not have permits to work, or (3) surveyed by CARP during the 1971 season. The primary areas falling outside these categories were those to the east, southeast, and southwest of the main survey zone. In these areas, approximately one transect was surveyed in every 9 square miles.

In addition to surveying random transects, several nonrandom transects were surveyed in specific areas where a greater sampling fraction was desired, such as along washes and in particular soil zones. The total area of these survey zones was small, and as a result we could expect this low intensity sample normally to include extremely small fractions of such areas as washes – which may be zones of high site density (F. Plog 1972:10).

A final component of the survey was block samples, and these samples can be grouped into two types. The first type comprised areas where local amateurs and forest service personnel had indicated pueblo sites existed. It was felt that these people would likely have knowledge of many of the largest sites in the area. Given the small percentage of the area that was surveyed, this was one way of getting a better sample of these sites in order to estimate their average size and frequency. A second type of block sample was the survey in the southeast corner of R. 19 E., T. 11 N., hereafter referred to as the Day Burn area. One disadvantage of transect samples is that they provide little information on settlement patterns over an area. Thus, it had been planned to survey an area of 2 to 3 square miles in order to obtain better information on settlement patterns and to obtain a sample similar to the block surveys in the Purcell–Larson area for comparative purposes. An initial random transect in the Day Burn area had suggested a high site density there. Three additional transects were then surveyed parallel to the first and spaced 0.5 mile apart. These transects also indicated a high site density. Because of the high site density and because problems of ground cover from pine needles had been eliminated by a fire in the area a month earlier, it was felt that the Day Burn would be a favorable area for obtaining information on settlement patterns.

The survey (hereafter referred to as the Pinedale Survey) thus consisted of three components: (1) stratified random transects, (2) nonrandom transects, and (3) block surveys. A discussion of site size in the Pinedale area will be presented in a later chapter.

Surface collection

A second aspect of the data collection during 1974 was surface collections of sites in the Purcell–Larson area and Pinedale area. This included both the collection of a sample of all artifacts on the surface of the sites and additional collections of rim sherds and painted ceramics. A systematic random sample of sherds from sites in the Purcell–Larson area was collected first in order to estimate surficial densities of artifacts on the sites. Such estimates are useful in comparing sites in different areas and will be discussed further below. Sites which were expected on the basis of survey notes to have 150 to 200 black-on-white sherds were chosen to be collected in this manner. Collections were made along transects 2 meters wide that ran from the approximate geographical center of the site to the site boundary at 30-degree intervals. The resultant twelve transects were further divided into 5-meter collection units along their lengths and every other 5-meter by 2-meter unit was collected. That is, the first, third, fifth, and so forth units were collected. For the 12 transects at each site, odd-numbered and even-numbered collection units were alternately collected. The primary disadvantage of this sampling procedure is that the center of the site is sampled more intensively than the periphery. However, this bias was constant between sites. The primary advantage of the sampling procedure was that two individuals could complete the sampling of one site in less than a day. After the sampling had been completed, all painted ceramics and all rim sherds on the surface of the sites were collected.

Sites in the Pinedale area with expected black-on-white counts of 150 to 200 sherds from the surface were also intensively collected, including all painted and rim sherds, in order to obtain large collections for analysis. While these sites were also sampled in order to obtain density estimates, serious sampling problems negate their use in this study. In contrast to the sites in the Purcell–Larson area, virtually all of the Pinedale area sites with large black-on-white collections had been disturbed through excavation or surface collection by amateurs. Thus, it is likely that amateur collectors removed artifacts from the surfaces of those sites. For an area near Pinedale, Lightfoot (1978) has shown that ceramic density is significantly lower on sites that have some indication of disturbance by amateur collectors than on sites without such indications. In addition, some of the material on the surface of these sites was material left from amateur excavations. On some areas of the sites, the amount of material deposited in this manner was large. Estimates of surface densities would thus be affected by this disturbance.

Excavation

The final stage of the data collection was limited excavation on several Purcell–Larson sites to obtain wood samples for tree-ring dating.

Previous excavation in the area had resulted in tree-ring dates for four sites from the area, three of which had good black-on-white collections. These sites all dated to the period between A.D. 1200 and 1300. Six more sites that were expected to date to this period on the basis of ceramics were tested in an attempt to add to the sample of well-dated sites from this period. It was felt that if enough sites that dated to different 25-year intervals within this 100-year period could be dated by tree rings, it would be possible to study design change through that period. Dates were obtained for four additional sites, providing a total of eight dated sites, five of which had large enough painted collections for design analysis.

This discussion has outlined the data base and the methods used to gather the evidence to be used in this study. In the next chapter, I will describe how the designs from the ceramics collected were analyzed.

4

Design classification

Despite the detailed studies of ceramic design variation that have been made by archaeologists, there has been little discussion of the methods that should be used in these analyses. In particular, insufficient attention has been given the question of how designs should be classified [the studies of Carlson (1970), Friedrich (1970), Redman (1977, 1978), and Washburn (1977, 1978) are important exceptions as will be noted later]. Analyses have focused on many different types of designs (or classificatory units) such as design elements or design motifs that have not been defined explicitly. The result has been an enormous amount of subjectivity in delimiting these units and, thus, a large amount of variation in what different individuals considered to be "design elements." Even terminology in describing a particular design varies tremendously. In summary, few people have critically evaluated our classifications to ask if they are reasonable ones. This is important, for as Hill (1970:17), among others, has argued, there is no reason to analyze intrasite or intersite variation in the distribution of items unless the items have been classified using sound methods.

Because there has been so little discussion of design classifications, it is difficult to describe how designs have been classified in most analyses. Many studies simply present a table showing drawings of different designs and their frequencies. In other cases, only minimal discussion is presented and many questions are left unanswered. For example, in his well-known study of ceramic designs at the Carter Ranch Site, Longacre (1964a:162–3) simply states that

> It was decided to work first with the smallest units of design and to combine units later if statistically relevant. For an artistic analysis, Shepard (1948; pp. 211, 291–292) has suggested that the use of design elements proves to be of little value, if not misleading. A design analysis of pottery should be made in terms of units of decoration such as bands or panels. For our analysis, however, we hoped

to define elements that would not be consciously selected from an artistic point of view. Rather, we hoped to isolate the smallest units of design that would be non-consciously selected based upon learning patterns within the social frame. The elements were defined from the sherds, the list growing as we progressed in the analysis.

However, Longacre does not state how we know what "the smallest units of designs" are or how we know which elements "would not be consciously selected from an artistic point of view." This deficiency in Longacre's study is one that has continued in many of the subsequent design studies. For example, Hill (1970:23) describes the manner in which the ceramic designs in his analysis were classified as follows:

The ceramic *design-elements* used in this study . . . could not be classified on the basis of an extant typology. All of the decorated sherds had to be examined individually and then divided into element-classes. This was done largely on the basis of *feel,* and design categories were chosen with the view to the isolation of microstyle differences among rooms within the pueblo [italics in original].

Given this lack of attention to design classifications and the seemingly arbitrary methods used in some cases, there is a need for explicit discussions of how we should classify ceramic designs. A fundamental assumption of the classification system used in this study is that classifying designs is no different than classifying other artifacts such as chipped or ground stone. Similar procedures should be followed in establishing a classification system. The fundamental units that must first be identified and explicitly defined are the attributes (for example, the location of notching on projectile points) and the attribute states (for example, side-notched or corner-notched) upon which the classification will be based, as Rouse (1960), Clarke (1968:134–45), and others have argued. Attributes in this study are equated with decisions, whether conscious or unconscious, made by the artisan during the manufacturing or decorating process (Clarke 1968:138; Deetz 1968b:223; Martin and Plog 1973:246; Rouse 1960:314). They also may be defined as "a logically irreducible character of two or more states, acting as an independent variable within a specific frame of reference – or system" (Clarke 1968:139).

One important aspect of attribute analysis is that the different attribute states, whether nominal or interval, must be a set of alternative choices, values or qualities (Clarke 1968:145) from which a prehistoric artisan selected one particular state at each decision-making point. That is, the attribute states must have the property of substitutability. For example, we would not compare the edge angle of one projectile point with the length of another. To do so would create chaos in any attempt to classify such artifacts. A particular edge angle and a particular artifact length are not substitutable; they are not mutually exclusive choices. The choice of the angle of the cutting edge and of the length of the artifact are *different decisions* that the manufacturer of the artifact had to make. This is a simple point, but it is one that is important in discussing previous design classifications.

Once the attributes to be used have been identified, spatial or temporal variation in an attribute can be measured by noting the frequency of different attribute states through space or through time. In addition, techniques to measure the association or correlation of different attribute states can be used and attempts made to isolate groups of attribute states that covary. Spatial and temporal variability in these more inclusive groups may then be examined. Thus, a second fundamental assumption of this study is that, whether ceramic designs or ground stone are being classified, we must first identify the attributes upon which the classification will be based in order to study some aspect of the variation.

Given this brief discussion of general classification procedures, some of the previous design classifications now will be evaluated in light of these remarks. Two major problems exist with many of the design classifications. First, the attributes upon which these studies are based, whether they are called design elements, design motifs, or some other term, often are not defined. This creates problems in interpreting the meaning of the variation in the units isolated. More importantly, however, it means that the studies cannot be replicated exactly. Without precise definitions, what I decide is a design element may be completely different from what someone else would call a design element. This variation between individuals has been demonstrated in one previous study. Tuggle (1970:72) had three people analyze the same set of ceramics and found that "the number of distinct elements and recorded occurrences varied greatly." He also found that similarity coefficients between two groups of data he had classified two months apart were lower than coefficients within a data set classified at one time (1970:72). The variation in design classifications between individuals also can be seen by simply comparing the design classifications developed by Hill, Longacre, Tuggle, and others.

The second problem with some previous classifications and analyses is that many of the studies have dealt with variation in the frequencies of design elements that do not have the property of substitutability. This problem can be illustrated by comparing design element numbers 6, 174, and 175 in Hill's classification, shown in

Figure 4.1. Design elements in Hill's (1970) classification system for Broken K Pueblo.

Figure 4.1. Element numbers 6 and 174 could be considered alternative states of the attribute of design shape or form. One design is a line and the other is a terraced figure. On prehistoric vessels from the American Southwest, we can often find terraces painted on one vessel in a location where lines are painted on other vessels. Thus, when choosing a particular form to paint on a vessel, terraced figures and lines were alternative choices for a prehistoric potter. However, element numbers 174 and 175 are not alternative states of the attribute of form; they are both lines and thus have the same form. They are alternative states of the attribute of size, one being a wider line than the other. The choice between these elements represents a *different decision* for the potter than the choice between element numbers 6 and 174. When comparing frequencies of element number 6 with element numbers 174 and 175 together, frequencies of alternative states of the single attribute of form are being compared. However, Hill did not analyze design frequencies in this way. In his factor analysis of design frequencies at Broken K, he considered the frequencies of all the design elements together. To use an analogy, we can compare lithic artifacts in terms of their edge angles or in terms of their lengths just as we could compare the designs labeled design element numbers 6, 174 and 175 in terms of their form *or* 174 and 175 in terms of their size. However, to compare the frequency of the *form* of one type of design (element number 6) with the frequencies of two different sizes of another type of design (design element numbers 174 and 175) is comparable to comparing the edge angles of lithic artifacts from one site with the lengths of such artifacts from another site. The actual situation is worse than this because some past researchers frequently have separated designs into design elements on the basis of a number of different attributes. This is why past typologies have been criticized because the differences between design elements are not equal, although they have been treated as such (Bartovics 1974:201); this can only create a meaningless morass.

The creation of higher level classificatory units, such as types or design elements, which are based on multiple attributes is a legitimate and frequently necessary step in the analytical process. However, such units must be based on strong patterns of covariation in the frequencies of the attribute states used to establish the types, and each type must be defined using the same set of attributes (though not attribute states). This was not done in the development of Hill's classification system. Thus, it is not surprising (as I have demonstrated elsewhere) that the localized clusters of designs that Hill felt he had isolated at Broken K do not exist (S. Plog 1976a). Unfortunately, the problem with Hill's classification is also a problem with many other systems such as the list of motifs and elements used by Washburn (1977:Table 15 and Figure 263) or the classifications of Clemen (1976), Connor (1968), Cronin (1962), Deetz (1965), Gerald (1975), Longacre (1970), Pollnac and Rowlett (1977), Tuggle (1970), and Wiley (1971), as they were done in a manner comparable to Hill's. The studies of Redman (1977, 1978) and Kintigh (1979), and Washburn's (1977, 1978) symmetry analysis in the American Southwest, Johnson's (1973) research in Iran, Redman's (1978) and Rubertone's (1978) work in Morocco, and Braun's (1977) analysis of ceramics from the midwestern United States are exceptions. Examination of Johnson's study and a preliminary copy of Redman's Cibola classification system, which he graciously provided, aided the development of the Chevelon design classification system.

The Chevelon design classification
On the basis presented, we can say that attributes are the basic units of design classifications. If so, what are the attributes of ceramic design that should be studied? Before answering this question, it first should be noted that attributes are needed that can be recorded for a collection of sherds. Unfortunately, many of the attributes that could be studied require that we have whole vessels or at least large sherds. Some of the attributes suggested by Carlson (1970) such as focus of decoration, layout, and pattern fall into this category. Symmetry analyses such as those done by Shepard (1948), Washburn (1977, 1978)

and other types of structural analyses such as Muller's (1973) also are difficult to carry out without whole vessels or large sherds. If design analyses are going to be useful in archaeological research for comparing individual sites, it is imperative that the techniques developed be applicable to sherds. Whole vessels or even large sherds are often not available from a single site in frequencies that will provide a sufficient sample size for analyses, particularly when only surface collections are available as in this study. A second consideration in choosing the attributes to be studied is Washburn's (1977:165) argument that the use of design symmetry classification provides a more "objective, standardized procedure" than do design element studies. As noted, the subjectivity and variation between individuals that has characterized the study of design features other than symmetry attributes is not inherent in such studies but is a result of the inadequate methods used. The attribute classification systems used in this study and in those of Redman (1977, 1978), for example, do not suffer from these problems. In addition, it does not seem wise to limit our studies to the relatively few symmetry attributes that can be studied on whole vessels or large sherds and not consider the large number of attributes that can be measured more frequently for a greater number of ceramic collections. Thus, our studies must concentrate on a wide variety of attributes that may be measured on sherds.

Given these considerations, the selection of specific attributes to be studied is dependent on the problem being investigated. The hypotheses I discussed earlier are phrased in terms of design variation in general rather than one specific aspect of that variation. Thus, in selecting attributes for the Chevelon design analysis, I attempted to use all attributes that previous studies in the region had shown to vary spatially or temporally. In addition, given the criticisms that I have made here and elsewhere (S. Plog 1976a, 1976b, 1978) of the use of ceramic design variation to infer characteristics of prehistoric social organization in the American Southwest and my proposal that other factors may explain part of that variation, I attempted to include the primary attributes that had been used implicitly to develop the classification systems used in those studies. Also, the results of an ethnographic study by Friedrich (1970) that focused on the relationship between design variation and social interaction were emphasized. The conclusions reached in that study will now be discussed.

Friedrich's study of a Tarascan pottery-making village in Mexico suggested three indicators that might be useful in measuring the intensity of interaction between potters. These indicators are: (1) the organization of spatial divisions, (2) the degree of subclass variation within design configuration classes, and (3) the function of a design element in a configuration (Friedrich 1970:338–9). Friedrich suggests these attributes because they are ignored in the decoding strategy that potters in the Tarascan village used to break down the design structure of vessels and thus the attributes are only diffused between potters in intense social interaction (Friedrich 1970:337).

The first of these attributes refers to the location of boundary markers between spatial divisions and to the types of boundary markers (Friedrich 1970:338). Unfortunately, these are attributes that are easy to measure when whole vessels are available, but can be measured infrequently when we have only sherds.

In regard to the second indicator, Friedrich notes several dimensions of subclass variation that may be measured. These include the number of different secondary design elements used with primary configurations, the manner in which these secondary elements are attached to primary configurations, the reduplication of primary elements, and the manner in which primary elements are joined in constructing configurations (Friedrich 1970:338–9). All of these different dimensions are attributes that have a reasonable probability of being measured on sherds and, thus, could be included as part of a ceramic design study.

Finally, Friedrich's third indicator of intensity of communication between potters, the function of a design element in a configuration, is also an attribute that may be measured on sherds. Using cross-hatching (illustrated later in Figure 4.3) as an example in her discussion of different element functions, Friedrich (1970:339) suggests analysis of the shapes of areas filled by cross-hatching and of "the kind of unit for which cross hatching may be substituted."

In addition to Friedrich's study, previous studies of designs on prehistoric ceramics from the American Southwest were examined for suggestions of attributes to be analyzed, as already noted. One source is the definitions and discussion of pottery types and design styles on prehistoric pottery from the Southwest such as Colton's (1953), Wasley's (1959), and Carlson's (1970). Carlson (1970:84–8) provides an extremely good description of these attributes. Motif form, motif composition, filler or secondary motifs, linearity (all illustrated in Figure 4.3), and line widths are some of the attributes discussed for which it is not necessary to have whole vessels or large sherds to measure.

Inasmuch as the attributes listed have been used to define pottery types, the alternative states of these attributes might be expected to vary primarily through time rather than through space. Ceramic attributes that have been used to define accepted spatial style groups (such as the Anasazi and Mogollon areas) in the American Southwest have been almost entirely attributes other than ceramic designs, such as type of temper and type of paint. Thus, there is less evidence to guide the choice of design attributes for studies atempting to define spatial groups. There are, however, a few studies that have utilized ceramics from within or near the Chevelon area and that have suggested that some of the design attributes listed might be useful in defining spatial groups of sites on the basis of ceramic designs. For example, Longacre (1962:163) has noted differences in design composition at approximately the same time period between the Pine Lawn Valley and Springerville areas near the Arizona–New Mexico border where solid and hatched designs were characteristic and the Hay Hollow Valley area in east-central Arizona where solid designs only were abundant. Also, Longacre has found that on black-on-white pottery from the Hay Hollow Valley stepped or terraced frets make up 40 percent of the designs and that "broad lines or stripes" were 15 percent (1964b:111–12). In contrast, Wilson (1969:310) noted that in the Heber region south of the Purcell–Larson area lines totaled 43 percent of the motif forms and frets were only 11.5 percent. There thus seem to be sharp differences between the Heber area and Hay Hollow Valley in the frequency of design forms. It should be noted, however, that these apparent differences between Longacre's and Wilson's figures may be more the result of differences in the definition of "design motifs" than a result of real design frequency differences. Definitions of such terms vary considerably between individuals. Also, Longacre only included broad lines in his figures, while Wilson (1969:310) included "broad, medium width, and fine parallel lines, and various combinations of these" in his figures.

Given the conclusions of Friedrich and the list of attributes that previous design analyses have dealt with, 21 design attributes initially were chosen to be recorded from the painted pottery to be analyzed. Basic to an understanding of how these attributes were measured is a distinction between primary units and secondary units (see Figure 4.2). In making this distinction, I am following the method of hierarchical analysis suggested by Friedrich (1970) and delineating two different levels of design organization. Primary and secondary units are defined in terms of unit *forms* and are basic geometrical shapes such as scrolls (both frets and scrolls will hereafter be referred to as scrolls in this study), stepped or terraced units, circles, rectangles, triangles, lines, and nongeometrical shapes such as life forms (Carlson 1970:85). In using the term *design unit* I am following the terminology of Carlson (1970:85); the comparable term in Friedrich's (1970:315) terminology would be "design element." I have chosen to avoid this latter term because it is used in many recent studies to denote designs of varying types and complexity. The distinction between secondary and primary forms can be stated in several ways. Carlson (1970:85) states that

> Primary motifs are those combinations of design units which are the strongest units in the pattern and form the

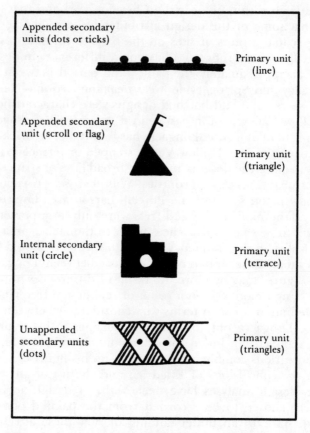

Figure 4.2. Examples of primary and secondary design forms.

basis thereof. Filler [or secondary] motifs are those units which are either included within the boundaries or appended to the borders of a primary motif, or are used to fill an area within the field of decoration which is not covered by the primary motifs.

Friedrich (1970:335) notes that "primary elements are painted first. Secondary elements are optional and, when they are added, their location in the configuration depends upon the kind of primary element used." In this study, the question of when a design form was primary or secondary was decided on the basis of one of two criteria. First, in some instances, such as the second design from the bottom in Figure 4.2, one of the forms (the circle) logically could not be used without the prior existence of the form (the terrace). In such cases, the former design was considered secondary and the latter design primary. With other designs, this decision was not so obvious. For example, in the bottom design in Figure 4.2, both the triangles and the circles or dots logically could be painted in isolation from each other rather than in combination. In practice, however, such was not the case. Those designs designated as primary forms in the Chevelon analysis occurred on vessels either in isolation from or in combination with other forms. In contrast, those designs considered to be secondary forms never occurred by themselves on vessels; they were painted only in conjunction with other forms. This latter pattern, then, allows the consistent, logical separation of primary from secondary forms when the entire design is visible. The distinction also can be illustrated, as shown in Figure 4.2. [Figure 2 in Friedrich (1970) also illustrates this distinction.]

In addition to the gross forms of secondary units, the specific form of ticking ("ticking" is illustrated in Figures 4.2 and 4.3), one type of secondary unit, was also recorded. This was done for two reasons. First, the type of ticking on black-on-white pottery is one of the important attributes distinguishing pottery types of Tusayan, Little Colorado, and Cibola White Wares. Second, preliminary sorting of the Chevelon ceramics suggested that ticking would be the most frequent type of secondary unit.

Attributes of primary and secondary units other than their form were also noted. The form of secondary units was recorded in terms of their location relative to primary units, that is: (1) appended from primary units, (2) within primary units, or (3) between primary units. Examples of a secondary form appended to and within a primary form are shown in Figures 4.2 and 4.3. The "mosquito-bar" design that is found on some pottery types in the American Southwest, in which several parallel lines are drawn between multiple primary forms such as interlocking terraces or triangles, is an example of a secondary form between primary units.

A second attribute initially recorded for both secondary and primary units was the manner in which each was combined with other units of the same form. Units may be separate, joined to each other, interlocked, or a combination of these (Carlson 1970:85). These combinations of primary units are referred to as "primary configurations" by Friedrich (1970:334–5) and as "primary motifs" by Carlson (1970:85). As noted earlier, Friedrich (1970:339) has suggested that the manner in which primary units are combined was one good indicator of the intensity of communication between potters in the Tarascan village of San Jose. In addition to recording the manner in which primary units were combined, the way in which primary motifs or primary units of different forms were combined was noted when possible.

A third attribute recorded for both primary and secondary units was whether or not the form was rectilinear or curvilinear. This distinction has primarily been important in defining types of Cibola

White Ware. Also, Longacre (1964b:113) has noted that the curvilinear motifs common on Tularosa Black-on-white, an abundant type in the Pine Lawn Valley and Reserve area are not found on Snowflake Black-on-white, a type found in the Hay Hollow Valley.

Finally, for primary units, the composition of the form was recorded. The most frequent states for this attribute were solid, hatched, checkerboard, and combinations of these, as shown in Figure 4.3. This is another type of subclass variation that Friedrich (1970:339) has suggested studying. Archaeological evidence concerning the spatial distributions of different types of composition has been indicated previously. When hatched designs were present, the type of hatching (simple hatching or cross-hatching), (see Figure 4.3) also was noted. No attempt was made to distinguish the different types of simple hatching that have been described by Wasley (1959:239–40) or Carlson (1970:85), because preliminary sorting indicated that it would be impossible to make this distinction on the majority of hatched sherds. For hatched designs, the width of hatching lines, the width of the space between the hatching lines, and the width of the framing lines (those lines that form the boundary of the space filled by hatching) were measured.

The final set of attributes recorded applied to primary lines only. The width of the lines, the shape of continuous lines (straight, zigzag, or wavy), the combination of lines (parallel, converging, intersecting), and the angle of intersecting lines (oblique or right angle) were noted. As indicated earlier, Wilson (1969:310) has found that simple lines were the most common forms on black-on-white ceramics from the Heber area. In addition, a study of black-on-white ceramics from the 1971 Chevelon survey suggested that the majority of designs consisted of lines (Cox and Mayer 1972:5); thus, it was felt that it would be important to record a variety of information on lines.

The design analysis
The attributes described were initially recorded by several individuals for a sample of over one thousand sherds from four different sites in the Purcell–Larson area for the purpose of determining which attributes would occur frequently enough to warrant coding on the remainder of the sherds to be analyzed. Both PGM and SShO sherds were included in the sample. In addition, sites of different dates were included in order to insure that attributes were not excluded simply because they were rare at one time. This analysis showed that some attributes were in fact too infrequent on sherds from all sites and from both pottery classes to continue recording. Secondary forms within primary units, types of ticking, the angle of line intersections, types of combinations of multiple primary units of the same form and of multiple primary units of different forms, and

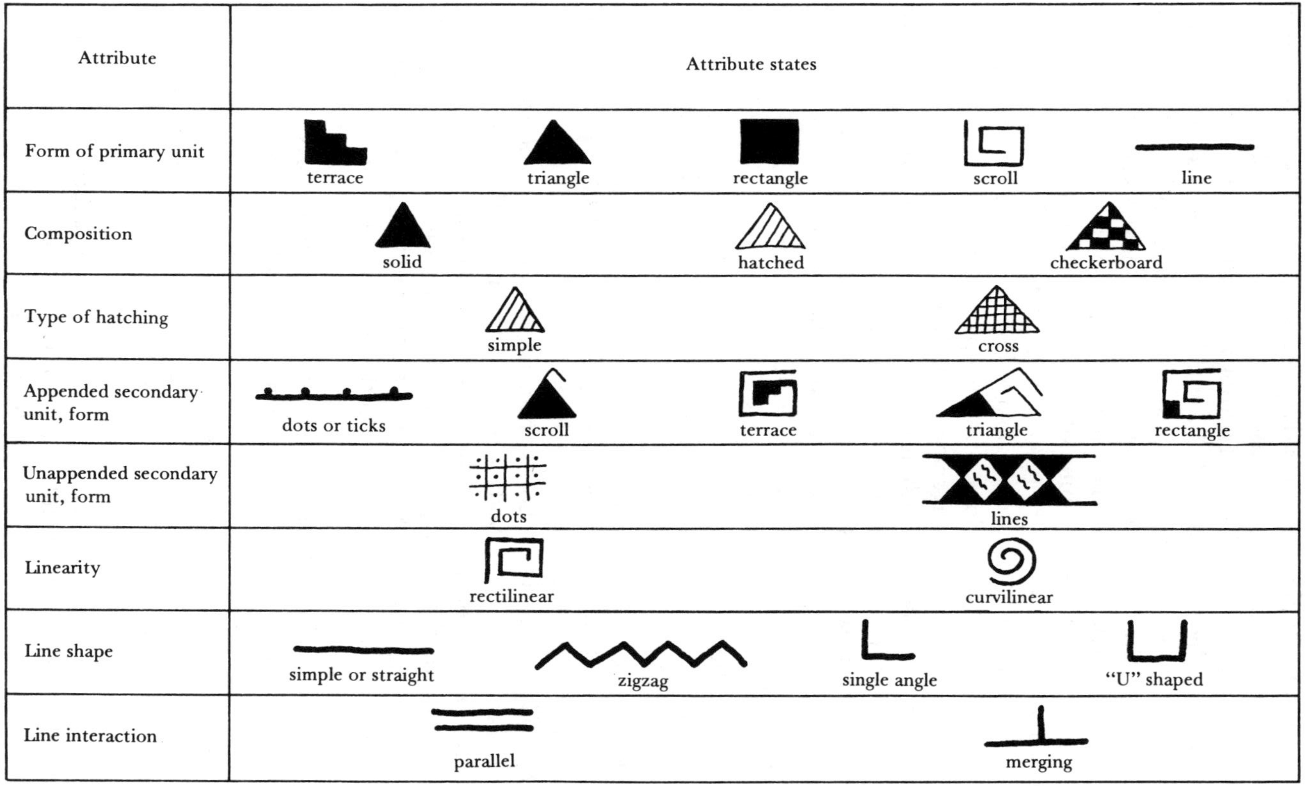

Attribute	Attribute states				
Form of primary unit	terrace	triangle	rectangle	scroll	line
Composition	solid	simple	hatched		
Type of hatching		simple	hatched	cross	checkerboard
Appended secondary unit, form	dots or ticks	scroll	terrace	triangle	rectangle
Unappended secondary unit, form		dots		lines	
Linearity		rectilinear		curvilinear	
Line shape	simple or straight	zigzag	single angle	"U" shaped	
Line interaction		parallel		merging	

Figure 4.3. Attributes with nominal states recorded for ceramic designs.

types of combinations of secondary units could not be coded on at least 90 percent and in most cases over 95 percent of sherds of both pottery classes from all sites. Furthermore, there was no patterned variation in the frequency of the attributes between sites, between vessel forms, between pottery classes, or through time. These attributes were, therefore, not measured in the next stage of analysis. The coded attributes with nominal states that were used in the final analysis and examples of some of the alternative states of these attributes that occur on Chevelon pottery are illustrated in Figure 4.3. In addition to these attributes, primary line width, width of hatching lines, width of framing lines, and the spacing between hatched lines were measured in the final stage of analysis.

Once the number of attributes to be recorded was reduced, sherds of both pottery classes from five sites were chosen to be analyzed for this study. These sites, CS 43, CS 412, CS 503, CS 690, and CS 734 (see Figure 3.2) were chosen because they were sites from which tree-ring dates, necessary for the study of temporal variability, had been obtained and because large samples of black-on-white pottery has been collected from the sites. One site with a tree-ring date, CS 470, was excluded because of the small sample of painted sherds that was collected from the site. A second site with tree-ring dates, CS 689, was excluded because the tree-ring dates suggest at least two occupations at the site. From CS 43, CS 412, and CS 734, all PGM and SShO body sherds were analyzed. All SShO body sherds and all PGM body sherds from bowls from CS 503 and CS 690 were analyzed. From the PGM body sherds from jars at the latter sites, a random sample of 200 sherds was chosen for the recording of all attributes. For the sherds not included in the random sample, only the types of primary forms, types of composition, types of appended secondary forms, types of unappended secondary forms, rectilinear versus curvilinear lines and scrolls, and types of hatching were coded. Thus, all attributes were recorded when possible for a total of 1481 PGM sherds and 698 SShO sherds from the five sites. A more limited number of attributes were coded for an additional 931 PGM sherds. The sample sizes for individual attributes are not in most cases equal to these figures, however, nor are they equal to each other. This is a result of the fact that all attributes could not be measured on every sherd. For the attribute of line width, for example, a line obviously had to be present on the sherd for the measurement to be made. Similarly, the type of hatching could only be recorded on those sherds with hatched forms.

In addition to the analysis of body sherds, all PGM and SShO rim sherds from 22 sites in the Purcell–Larson area were analyzed in order to record one attribute, the presence or absence of painted designs on the rim of the vessel. This attribute was included because

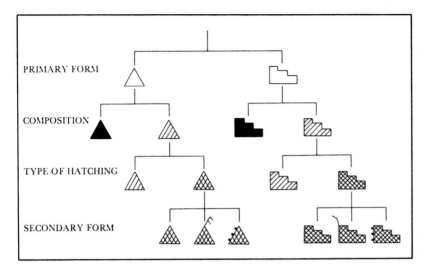

Figure 4.4. Tree-diagram illustrating hierarchical nature of design classification system. Each level of the diagram represents a different decision made by the prehistoric artisan.

preliminary examination of the rim sherds had suggested differences between PGM and SShO sherds in the frequency of decorated rims. A total of 816 PGM rims and 361 SShO rims were analyzed. Finally, some design attributes on rims from PGM jars were measured in order that designs on jar rims could be compared with designs on jar bodies. Only a few attributes such as type of primary form and type of composition were coded, however. Because of the low frequencies of jar rim sherds, only attributes that could be coded on almost every rim sherd warranted consideration.

Summary

The classification system used to analyze ceramic designs on Chevelon pottery is hierarchical in that it emphasizes alternative choices made by the potter at different points in the process of decorating a vessel. A decision on whether to paint a solid triangle or a hatched triangle is different from and follows the decision concerning what type of form (triangle, terrace, etc.) to paint, as illustrated in Figure 4.4. There are, thus, a series of steps in the decorative process at which different decisions must be made. Most previous design classifications have not recognized these as different decisions and have, thus, analyzed relative frequencies of different design elements that were not alternative choices. Previous classification procedures also have not been explicitly described, resulting in subjective and unreplicable classifications. The classification system that I have briefly described here is suggested as one that does not suffer from either of these deficiencies.

5

Ceramic exchange

A brief discussion of the possible causes of ceramic exchange and of
the possible importance of exchange in explaining spatial variability
in ceramic designs was presented in Chapter 2. In this chapter, I will
discuss briefly methods for identifying the exchange of materials
and then will discuss in greater detail ceramic exchange in the prehistoric Southwest. Two primary topics will be considered in the
latter discussion: First, the evidence concerning the frequency of
ceramic exchange in the Southwest as known from previous studies
will be summarized. Second, a specific case will be examined – the
significance of ceramic exchange as an explanation of design variability in the Chevelon drainage area.

Methods of studying ceramic exchange
Two primary types of data and several different methods of collecting that data are useful for the study of prehistoric ceramic exchange systems. Only recently, however, have some of these types of
analyses been widely available. Shepard has argued that information
on the mineral content of ceramic vessels obtained through optical
mineralogy (petrographic analysis) or X-ray diffraction analysis is
the most useful data (1971:x). She notes that such analyses provide
information on the materials used by the potter and the methods
used, and also may provide clues concerning the sources of the
materials. For the specific geographic location of these sources to be
identified, studies of the spatial distribution of geological materials
should be done in conjunction with the mineralogical analysis. Interpretation of the importance of the presence of a particular mineral
in a type of pottery will vary depending on whether or not the
natural distribution of the mineral in space is very limited or is also
very broad.

Chemical characterization of ceramics through methods such as
neutron activation analysis, atomic absorption analysis, and X-ray
flourescence spectrometry are valuable types of analyses and have
been used with increasing frequency in exchange studies. Differ-

ences between ceramics in the abundance of particular chemical elements may be the result of use of different types of raw materials in the production of the vessels. Thus, analysis of chemical variation in ceramics may lead to the isolation of groups of ceramics made in different areas. However, chemical differences also simply may reflect variation in the proportions of the raw materials such as the amount of the temper added to the clay (Shepard 1971:x). Thus chemical analyses are most useful when done in conjunction with mineralogical analysis, which can aid in determining the causes of any observed chemical variation.

General summaries of other aspects of both mineralogical and chemical analyses are presented by Shepard (1971) and Peacock (1970), among others. As noted earlier, the use of such methods has resulted in the demonstration of the prehistoric exchange of a large number of ceramic vessels in some areas of the world. The extent to which these methods have been used to measure the amount of ceramic exchange in the American Southwest prehistorically will now be discussed.

Studies of ceramic exchange in the American Southwest
Southwestern archaeologists have often assumed that ceramic exchange was not common prehistorically in the region. This has been particularly true of those individuals who have recently studied prehistoric ceramic design variation. In all but a few of these studies, the possibility that the ceramics that were analyzed were not made locally is not even mentioned (Clemen 1976; Connor 1968; Gerald 1975; Hill 1970; Kintigh 1979; Leone 1968; Redman 1978; Washburn 1977; Washburn and Matson 1980; Wiley 1971). The analyses of Longacre (1964a, 1964b, 1970) and Tuggle (1970:108–14) are the only exceptions. Unfortunately, while Tuggle did discuss ceramic exchange, his study was not done in conjunction with any type of analysis in order to test the hypothesis that the ceramics were not locally made. Longacre did have 20 black-on-white and black-on-red sherds analyzed petrographically and also analyzed several hundred using a binocular microscope (1964b:119–20). He states that "these analyses indicated that all the sherds examined were tempered with sherds and that they were all composed of the same paste (kind of clay)" (1964b:120). This conclusion implies that all the ceramics were made locally and Longacre used this assumption in his analysis of the Carter Ranch Site ceramic designs. However, neither the original analysis (Porter 1976) nor a reanalysis of the same thin sections (Garrett 1976) support the conclusion that the paste of all the sherds was the same. Porter's notes (a copy of which was kindly provided by Dr. Porter) and Garrett's reanalysis of the original thin sections plus thin sections of three additional sherds of both Snowflake Black-on-

white (Snowflake variety) and Snowflake Black-on-white (Hay Hollow variety) (Longacre 1964b), from the Carter Ranch Site suggest that the two types are characterized by different types of clays. For example, the Hay Hollow variety sherds had greater frequencies of ferromagnesium minerals, plagioclase, and igneous rock fragments than the Snowflake variety sherds (Garrett 1976). Thus, it should not be concluded that all the sherds from the Carter Ranch Site were locally made.

While design analysts have failed to consider the possibility of ceramic exchange, other researchers have dealt with the intensity and spatial extent of ceramic exchange in the prehistoric Southwest. Some of these analyses have simply considered the spatial distribution of a particular pottery type and assumed that occurrences of the type outside of the area where it was assumed to have been made indicate exchange (Schaefer 1969). However, no positive demonstration that trade occurred is made in this type of study. The spatial distribution of a type of pottery is one variable that should be considered in attempting to determine where a particular type was manufactured. Spatial discontinuities in the distribution of a type or decreasing frequencies of a type with increasing distance from a particular site or area may be the result of exchange. However, these spatial patterns also may be the result of other processes (Martin and Plog 1973:256). Without independent evidence, we can only guess as to the actual cause.

There have been a few published analyses that have obtained mineralogical information in order to test hypotheses concerning ceramic exchange between different regions in the Southwest in a rigorous manner. These are the studies of Shepard (1939, 1942, 1965), Warren (1969), and Danson and Wallace (1956), and I will summarize briefly the results of these studies. It is important to consider these results because they provide the only good data for drawing conclusions on the spatial extent and intensity of prehistoric Southwestern ceramic exchange.

The first petrographic analysis of Southwestern pottery was done by Shepard (1942, 1965). She initially analyzed glaze-painted sherds from the site of Pecos in the Upper Pecos River Valley in northern New Mexico and then expanded the study to include glaze-painted sherds from other sites in the Rio Grande Valley. The original goal of Shepard's study was not to study ceramic exchange but simply was to test the utility of optical petrology in identifying mineral inclusions in pottery (Shepard 1965:68). The result of Shepard's study of the Pecos pottery was the conclusion that the tempering material in "a significant proportion of the pottery" could not have been obtained locally (1965:68). The petrographic analysis in conjunction with knowledge of the natural distributions of minerals has indicated that a considerable amount of pottery had been imported by the inhabitants of Pecos. Furthermore, the analysis of glaze-painted sherds from other Rio Grande Valley sites indicated ceramic exchange was common in the area. Shepard even suggested that during one time period glaze-painted wares were being produced only in one area, the Galisteo Basin, and that production of the ware was centrally controlled (Shepard 1965:81).

Shepard argues that simple analysis of the surface characteristics of pottery would not have discovered the extensive exchange of pottery in the Rio Grande Valley (1965:86). Kidder has made a detailed study of design and rim attributes of the glaze-paint wares of Pecos which has not indicated that the ceramics were not made at the pueblo (Kidder and Kidder 1917; Shepard 1965:66). Shepard (1965:86) argues that

> Extensive intraregional trade results in such an intermingling of types in different districts that outward appearances of the pottery give the archaeologist no clue to the actual centers of production. In some instances, relative frequency of occurrence of wares may actually create an erroneous impression, as was so plainly demonstrated in the case of production in the northern districts of the Glaze-paint area.

Thus, conclusions concerning ceramic exchange should not be based on surface characteristics alone.

Warren's (1969) study of ceramic exchange also involved petrographic analysis of glaze-painted sherds from the Rio Grande Valley. She analyzed Glaze C and D pottery, which dates to approximately A.D. 1425 to 1515. The analysis of the tempering materials in the pottery in conjunction with the analysis of the surface color and designs, and the spatial distributions of the Glaze C and D types and natural sources of tempering materials, made it possible to identify sherds made at one village, the pueblo of Tonque (1969:36). Pottery made at this one village was extensively traded throughout the Rio Grande Valley.

> During the fifteenth and sixteenth centuries, the skilled potters of Tonque Pueblo . . . supplied well over half and sometimes nearly all of the glaze decorated pottery used in contemporary villages . . . The Zia villages, which have one of the longest and most consistent records of pottery making in the Rio Grande, obtained almost one-third of their ceramics from Tonque during this period. At Gran Quivira, eighty miles to the south, between twenty and thirty-five percent of the Glaze C and D pottery . . . was imported from Tonque. Tonque pottery was also traded

to more distant villages, including the Zuni pueblos 150 miles to the west, and to the Plains Indians to the east in Texas, Kansas, and Oklahoma [Warren 1969:36].

A third petrographic analysis was Danson and Wallaces' (1956) study of Gila Polychrome, a type which is widely distributed through southern Arizona, western New Mexico, and Northern Mexico. Some individuals have proposed that Gila Polychrome was locally manufactured throughout its distribution, while others have suggested that it was widely traded. To test the hypothesis that the type was widely traded, five sherds from each of four sites in southern Arizona and from one area of eastern New Mexico were analyzed petrographically. The analysis showed "that all the sherds from one area tend to have the same basic mineral components and that they differ as a group from the others" (Danson and Wallace 1956:182). This evidence suggested that Gila Polychrome was locally manufactured in the areas considered.

An additional petrographic study by Shepard dealt with sherds from Morris' (1939) work in the La Plata district of southwestern Colorado and northwestern New Mexico. Although only a few definite indications of ceramic exchange were identified, Shepard's analysis revealed a complex situation in regard to types of temper and paint used during the occupation of the area (Shepard 1939:249–87). This situation was particularly true during Pueblo III when ceramics decorated with mineral paint and tempered with sherds and ceramics decorated with organic paint and tempered with crushed rocks were found in the area. The explanation of the co-occurrence of the two types in the area was not clear and Shepard suggested a number of hypotheses to explain it (1939:285–6). This petrographic analysis thus did not indicate extensive ceramic exchange prehistorically in the La Plata district.

In conjunction with her analysis of the sherds from the La Plata area, Shepard also studied sherds from stratigraphic tests II and IV at Pueblo Bonito in the Chaco Canyon of northwestern New Mexico. Shepard's petrographic analysis revealed two types of temper in the Pueblo Bonito pottery that were not found locally. These tempering materials were sanidine basalt, for which the nearest known source is 80 kilometers (50 miles) west of Chaco Canyon in the Chuska Mountains, and andesite, for which the nearest source is 24 kilometers (15 miles) from Pueblo Bonito (Judd 1954:182). However, Shepard felt that the closest source of andesite was not the source of the tempering material in the sherds and that the andesite-tempered pottery may have been imported from the La Plata region (Shepard in Judd 1954:237). It was felt that the importation of the andesite-tempered pottery, which made up 4 percent of all sherds in stratigraphic tests

II and IV, was likely because "the principal occurrence of andesite in Bonito pottery is in Mesa Verde Black-on-white sherds which have, on stylistic grounds, been recognized as intrusives" (Shepard in Judd 1954:237). These andesite-tempered, black-on-white sherds were decorated with organic paint, in contrast to the mineral-painted black-on-white sherds that were most common at Pueblo Bonito and that were tempered with sherds.

While the proportion of andesite tempered pottery was low at Pueblo Bonito, this was not true of the ceramics tempered with sanidine basalt. This type of temper occurred in 22 percent of the sherds in stratigraphic tests II and IV (Shepard in Judd 1954:237) and increased in frequency through time. Judd (1954:182) states

> If the presence of sanidine basalt temper in pottery exhumed at Pueblo Bonito identifies the pottery as foreign, then Bonitian women were annually becoming more and more dependent upon others for their pots and pans. Of nine sherds from the lowest level (K) of Test II, three are plain-surfaced culinary ware and one of them is tempered with sanidine basalt. Another fragment, that of an unpainted pitcher or olla, is tempered with the same rock. Nearly 14 percent of all sherds in Stratum H, or 17.3 percent of the culinary ware only, are likewise tempered with sanidine basalt. For Stratum F the percentages are, respectively 24 and 53.3; for C, 29.9 and 66.6. Thus as old Bonitian rubbish accumulated, pottery tempered with sanidine basalt, both cooking pots and tableware, was gaining in local favor.

Overall, sanidine basalt-tempered pottery made up 40.7 percent of all culinary ware fragments, 60.2 percent of all black-on-white sherds with organic paint in strata C through K of test II, and was the "dominant temper" in corrugated pottery that initially appeared in stratum C (Judd 1954:183). In test IV, which was temporally later than test II, the proportion of sanidine basalt temper in corrugated and plainware from different strata varied from 55 percent to 87 percent (Shepard 1939:280).

Thus, if sanidine basalt-tempered pottery was imported to Pueblo Bonito, it made up a large proportion of all the pottery found at Pueblo Bonito and, in particular, a high proportion of the culinary (unpainted) vessels. Shepard argues that trade is the most logical explanation of the presence of the sanidine basalt-tempered pottery at Pueblo Bonito because of the distance to the closest source and because sanidine basalt "has been found as the principal temper in the Bennett Peak district east of the Chuska Mountains"; the only known source of sanidine basalt is in that locality (Shepard in Judd

1954:236). Although it has been suggested that sanidine basalt may have been procured near the Chaco Canyon sites (Everett 1970), a recent examination of numerous sites in Chaco Canyon and surrounding areas did not "reveal a single artifact or rock of sanidine basalt" (Windes 1977:286). Given the frequency in Pueblo Bonito and other Chaco Canyon sites of pottery tempered with sanidine basalt, Windes (1977:288) estimates that thousands of these ceramic vessels were traded into the Canyon.

In addition to these mineralogical analyses, a few studies of the chemical composition of Southwestern ceramics have been carried out. One of these studies, Wait's (n.d.) chemical characterization of black-on-white ceramics from the Chevelon area, will be discussed later. In the only other study which has examined the chemical composition of Southwestern ceramics in order to test for possible exchange ties, Deutchman (1979) used neutron activation analysis to characterize black-on-white ceramics from northeastern Arizona, particularly the Black Mesa area. Her analysis suggested possible ceramic exchange between the populations of Black Mesa and surrounding areas, but the results were not clear-cut.

These petrographic studies indicate several things. First, and most important, they suggest that ceramic exchange was common prehistorically in the American Southwest and that large numbers of vessels were moved between areas. The analysis of Warren (1969) and Shepard's Rio Grande Valley (1942, 1965) and Chaco Canyon (1939; Judd 1954) studies, three of the five intensive petrographic analyses that have been done in the Southwest, support this conclusion. These studies should have changed our ideas about ceramic production in the prehistoric Southwest. As Kidder (Kidder and Shepard 1936:xxiii) has stated.

> We are faced by the necessity for a drastic rearrangement of ideas regarding the status of the ceramic industry, not only at Pecos, but throughout the Southwest. It has always been assumed that pottery was one of the regular household tasks of every Pueblo woman; that each town was in this regard self-sufficient. But if whole classes of pottery . . . were imported, we must postulate an extraordinary volume of trade and allow for a compensating outward flow of other commodities. Furthermore, we must believe that the production of vessels at the source of supply was much greater than was needed for home consumption, in other words, that rudimentary commercial manufacturing was practiced.

However, the lack of concern with ceramic exchange in the design studies previously discussed support the conclusion that the results of the petrographic studies have not changed ideas concerning the frequency of ceramic trade. The possibility that ceramic exchange was frequent almost seems to have been regarded as "something of archaeological heresy" (Judd 1954:235).

The petrographic analyses also indicate that other common assumptions concerning ceramic exchange are often incorrect. First, it has been argued that more portable vessels such as small jars and, in particular, bowls that can be nested within each other were primarily traded when exchange did occur (H. S. Colton 1973:88–9; Colton and Hargrave 1937:27; McGregor 1965:101; Whittlesey 1974; Wilson 1969:312). However, in two of the areas where frequent ceramic exchange has been demonstrated, ollas (Warren 1969:36) and corrugated jars (Judd 1954:183) were the most frequent form exchanged. Second, it is often assumed that only decorated vessels were traded (H. S. Colton 1973:88; McGregor 1965:101). McGregor argues that this is a result of "their beauty and expert workmanship, as well as their smaller size" (1965:101). A prevalent argument in archaeological reports is that a particular type of painted pottery is made locally because it has the same temper as the dominant type of corrugated or plain ware pottery. Evidence already summarized does indicate that exchange of decorated pottery may have been more common, but only Shepard's Pueblo Bonito and La Plata district studies even included the analysis of culinary wares. The large number of corrugated vessels imported into Pueblo Bonito and ethnographic examples of similar occurrences (Ford 1972a:41) again suggest that it should not automatically be assumed that undecorated pottery was always locally made.

Thus, the petrographic analyses of prehistoric Southwestern ceramics suggest that a number of common assumptions about ceramic exchange often are incorrect. It is important that more studies of ceramic exchange be made and a necessity that they accompany stylistic analyses. Moreover, in conjunction with stylistic analyses, we must test the hypothesis that ceramic exchange was infrequent rather than assume that the hypothesis is correct. Otherwise, we could be making arguments about types of residence groups on the basis of pottery that was not even made in the community in question.

While it is important to have additional petrographic studies in order to study the frequency of prehistoric ceramic exchange, it should also be recognized that exchange may be common in areas where petrographic analyses would not suggest that it was. For petrographic studies to indicate exchange, it is necessary that the area where the pottery is manufactured and the area where the pottery is found be geologically different in some way. If the areas are not different geologically, then the types of available temper and the types of minerals that would be found in the clay would be the same in the two areas. Thus, ceramic exchange that occurred between geologically similar areas, between different communities in a single area, or between households within a single community would not be detected petrographically. In fact, it is doubtful if the latter two types of exchange could be detected in any way, except possibly through analysis of chemical composition.

Such exchange is common ethnographically in the Southwest, for example, in the village ceramic specialization among the Hopi. During the prehistoric period, McGregor (1965:101) has suggested that it is possible that only a few families or villages made some types of pottery and traded it to populations in surrounding areas. However, other than Shepard's and Warren's analyses of ceramics from the Rio Grande Valley area, there is little direct evidence available to support exchange between different communities within a small area and there is no documentation of ceramic trade between families within a village. For example, Longacre (1966) has proposed that there was intravillage specialization in the production of some tools at Broken K Pueblo, but does not discuss ceramics. Reports of potter's "tool kits" such as those found at Show Low Ruin (Haury and Hargrave 1931) or at Four-mile Ruin (Fewkes 1904) are rare in the literature, a pattern that should not occur if each household made its own pottery; but this is only a very indirect indicator of possible specialization in production. In addition, data from a site in northeastern Arizona reported by Beals, Brainerd, and Smith (1945) does suggest some specialization in production. They note (1945:138) that of the 50 graves excavated at the site, only 5 had pottery-making materials and tools as part of the associated grave goods, whereas a larger number had tools used for a variety of other activities. They suggest that only about one-third to one-half of the adult women who lived at the site manufactured pottery. Given this slim evidence and the lack of attention given to the question of specialization in the production of ceramic vessels prehistorically in the American Southwest, a blanket assumption that specialization did not occur is not warranted. The question of prehistoric community and intracommunity specialization should remain open rather than be closed without discussion.

The Chevelon analysis
As we have seen, it is important in analyzing pottery to determine whether or not it was made locally when we are attempting to explain ceramic design variability in an area. The analysis of ceramic designs from the Chevelon area involved the two black-on-white pottery classes, SShO and PGM, which were most abundant during the occupation of the area. Therefore, a petrographic analysis of these two classes was done by Ms. Elizabeth Garrett in conjunction

with the study of ceramic designs. This petrographic information along with other relevant data such as the spatial distribution of the two classes, their chemical composition, and the stylistic differences between the two classes will now be discussed.

Spatial distribution

We noted previously that SShO and PGM are made differently. Although they both are tempered with sherds, the sherd temper in SShO appears as white flecks against the dark gray paste, and the sherd temper in PGM shows up as dark flecks against a white paste. This difference suggests (but does not demonstrate) that SShO may have been made from a carbonaceous clay and that PGM was made from a low carbonaceous clay (Shepard 1953:180–1). The classes of SShO and PGM are also different in surface finish and type of paint used, as noted. SShO has a thin white slip that was polished either on both the interior and exterior of the vessel or on at least the surface that was to be painted. PGM was not slipped but the surface was polished. Also, SShO was decorated with an organic paint and PGM was decorated with a mineral paint.

It was noted too that SShO and PGM correspond to Little Colorado White Ware and Cibola White Ware, respectively, in the traditional Southwestern pottery classification. H. S. Colton (1955) indicates that Little Colorado White Ware was manufactured in the Little Colorado River Valley of Arizona from the Petrified Forest National Monument to the San Francisco Mountain area and was traded to the south to populations in the Tonto Basin, Verde Valley, and upper Gila drainage. He also proposed that Walnut Black-on-white, a type of Little Colorado White Ware, was made in the area east of Flagstaff and west of the Chevelon drainage, between Canyon Padre and Canyon Diablo (1941:55). Gumerman and Skinner (1968:185) have described the distribution of "pure" Little Colorado White Ware sites. They place the southern boundary just south of the Little Colorado River from the town of Holbrook to the area northwest of Leupp. The eastern boundary follows a line drawn almost due north from Holbrook, while the northern boundary falls just south of the Hopi Villages at the southern foot of Black Mesa; this area is shown in Figure 5.1. Gumerman and Skinner (1968:197) also note that large amounts of Little Colorado White Ware are found in the Flagstaff area on the west and that on the east there is a ceramic transition zone between Holbrook, where primarily Little Colorado White Ware is found, and the Petrified Forest, where more Cibola White Ware is found. Wilson (1969:301) notes that Little Colorado White Ware was the most common black-on-white ware in his Anderson Mesa and Upper Canyon Diablo localities and that it was found in approximately equal frequencies with Snowflake Black-on-white (a Cibola

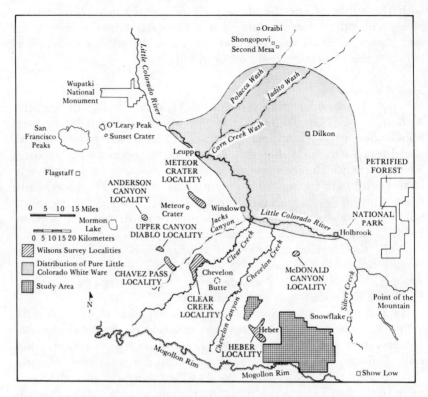

Figure 5.1. Distribution of pure Little Colorado White Ware sites according to Gumerman and Skinner (1968).

White Ware) in the Clear Creek and McDonald Canyon localities; these areas are also shown in Figure 5.1. He further notes that the distribution of Little Colorado White Ware extends into the Heber locality. He has proposed that Little Colorado White Ware was not manufactured in any of these localities, but rather was imported (1969:298–99, 301–2). He suggests (1969:302) that the ware was manufactured east of the area suggested by Colton. His discussion of the center of distribution of Little Colorado White Ware indicates that the eastern boundary is in the area around Holbrook and the Petrified Forest and that the western boundary "falls short of Leupp, Arizona" (Wilson 1969:305). This area is within the distribution of pure Little Colorado White Ware sites as indicated by Gumerman and Skinner.

In summary, the area in which Little Colorado White Ware is most dominant in terms of the proportions of different white wares is the area north of the Little Colorado River between Leupp and Holbrook. It is thus directly north of the Chevelon drainage. The CARP surveys, as noted before, have located pure Little Colorado White Ware sites throughout most of the Chevelon drainage, but at least 80 percent of the sites in the drainage area have large percentages of Cibola White Ware also. Thus, the Chevelon and Pinedale areas fall outside of the areas where a large percentage of the sites have Little Colorado White Ware as the dominant black-on-white ware. However, along with Flagstaff and other areas to the west, Chevelon is where large numbers of Little Colorado White Ware sherds are found.

The spatial distribution of Cibola White Ware, which is equivalent to PGM in the Chevelon ceramic classification, is much broader than that of Little Colorado White Ware. It is found as far east as the Rio Grande Valley in New Mexico and as far north as southwestern Colorado and southeastern Utah (Martin and Plog 1973:254). Rather than describe the limits of its entire distribution I will concentrate only on the relationship of Chevelon to the western and northern boundaries of the distribution. There is no question that Cibola White Ware was the dominant black-on-white ware prehistorically over a large area to the east of Chevelon. The work of the Southwest Archaeological Expedition of the Field Museum in east-central Arizona in the Hay Hollow Valley, the Vernon area, the Springerville area, and in west-central New Mexico in the Pine Lawn Valley provides the evidence (Martin et al. 1962, 1964; Martin, Longacre, and Hill 1967). Nor is there any question that the distribution of Cibola White Ware extends south of Chevelon. The work of the University of Arizona in the Grasshopper area supports this conclusion (Tuggle 1970).

The distribution of Cibola White Ware extends no farther north and west than Chevelon. As noted earlier, Little Colorado White Ware is dominant north of the drainage. Thus, the Chevelon area is at the extreme northern limits of the distribution of Cibola White Ware in east-central Arizona. In regard to the western distribution limits, it again appears that Chevelon is near the boundary. Wilson (1969:311) found that Cibola White Ware was rare east of Clear Creek. In addition, the association of Cibola White Ware with Alameda Brown Ware in Clear Creek (in contrast to its association with other brown wares in the Heber locality) along with the greater frequency of Cibola White Ware bowls relative to jars in Clear Creek (as opposed to findings at Heber) led Wilson to propose that Cibola White Ware was imported into the Clear Creek region (1969:12). He thus suggests that the Chevelon drainage is the westernmost area where Cibola White Ware was locally manufactured.

To summarize this discussion, Chevelon is just south of the area where Little Colorado White Ware is the dominant black-on-white pottery. Also, the former area lies just within the northern and western limits of the area where Cibola White Ware is abundant and, for the time period between A.D. 1200 and 1300, predominate. On the basis of these distributions and the associated plain ware and corrugated types, Wilson (1969:302, 306, 311) has suggested that Little Colorado White Ware was imported into the Chevelon area and that Cibola White Ware was locally made. Additional evidence relevant to this hypothesis will now be examined.

Mineral composition

Shepard has argued that mineralogical data are the most useful information for studying ceramic exchange. To obtain mineralogical information on the PGM and SShO sherds, thin sections of 32 SShO sherds and 20 PGM sherds from the Purcell–Larson area were made and analyzed petrographically by Elizabeth Garrett of the department of geology at Western Michigan University. Initial examination of these thin sections revealed differences between the two ceramic classes in their composition. The PGM sherds had higher frequencies of microcline and quartz and lower frequencies of ferromagnesium minerals, such as biotite, pyroxene, and hornblende, and igneous rock fragments. The grain size of the orthoclase (untwinned feldspar) inclusions was larger in the PGM sherds.

In order to quantify these differences, a systematic sample of counts of clay matrix, temper, and minerals was taken from 300 points on each of 18 SShO and 18 PGM thin sections. Three sherds from each of six sites (CS numbers 43, 412, 470, 503, 690, and 734) from the Purcell–Larson area were selected in order to include sites with a wide temporal range. For each sherd, the percentage frequencies of clay matrix, sherd temper, and any minerals present were calculated. The average frequency of each constituent for the two pottery classes are presented in Table 5.1. These figures confirm the conclusions from the qualitative analysis. The SShO sherds have higher average frequencies of clay matrix, twinned feldspar, igneous rock, ferromagnesium minerals, opaques, and alterates, and the PGM sherds have higher average frequencies of quartz, chert, untwinned feldspar, microcline, and sherd temper. Igneous rock and alterates were completely absent from the PGM thin sections, and microcline was absent from the SShO thin sections. The statistical significance of these differences was tested using contingency tables. For clay matrix, quartz, chert, untwinned feldspar, twinned feldspar, and sherd temper, a median test (Dixon and Massey 1969:351) was used. The presence or absence of microcline, igneous rock, ferromagnesium minerals, opaques, and alterates were used to construct the contingency tables for these constituents. The chi-square values calculated from these tables are also presented in Table 5.1. These values show that the differences between SShO and PGM for quartz, microcline, sherd temper, igneous rock, ferromagnesium minerals, and alterates

Table 5.1. *Means and standard deviations (in percentages) by ceramic class of ceramic constituents identified by petrographic analysis*

Constituent	SShO			PGM			Chi-square
	Mean	Standard deviation	Sample size	Mean	Standard deviation	Sample size	
Clay matrix	85.7	2.8	18	81.7	5.1	18	2.78
Quartz	2.3	1.0	18	4.4	1.9	18	9.00[a]
Chert	0.5	0.5	18	0.9	0.7	18	0.45
Untwinned feldspar	1.6	0.7	18	2.4	1.2	18	1.78
Twinned feldspar	0.7	0.4	18	0.5	0.6	18	1.78
Microcline	0.0	0.0	18	0.3	0.4	18	7.88[a]
Sherd temper	7.2	2.6	18	9.6	2.3	18	5.44[b]
Volcanic rock	0.8	0.6	18	0.0	0.0	18	22.40[a]
Ferro-magnesium	0.5	0.4	18	0.1	0.1	18	13.61[a]
Opaques	0.2	0.3	18	0.1	0.3	18	2.81
Alterates	0.6	1.2	18	0.0	0.0	18	7.88[a]

[a]Statistically significant at the 0.01 level.
[b]Statistically significant at the 0.05 level.

are statistically significant at the 0.05 level. These tests suggest that SShO vessels were not made with the same clay as that used to make PGM vessels. It should be noted, however, that these tests are not independent since the figures used are relative frequencies calculated from closed arrays. Also, for the contingency tables for microcline and alterates, the expected frequencies for two cells (the intersections of the rows and columns in the contingency table, e.g., the number of PGM sherds with microcline frequencies greater than the median) in each table were both 4, whereas in such contingency tables not more than 20 percent of the expected frequencies should be less than 5 (Dixon and Massey 1969:238).

Perhaps the most important difference in the mineral composition of the two classes is the presence of igneous rock fragments in all the SShO sherds and their absence from all of the PGM thin sections. There are no volcanic deposits in the Purcell–Larson area, nor are there any in the areas south of Purcell–Larson that drain into Purcell and Larson Draws. The closest volcanic deposit to Purcell–Larson is Chevelon Butte, which is an average of about 22.5 kilometers (14 miles) from the Purcell–Larson sites considered in this study. Volcanic deposits are abundant further to the west and east and also to the north in the Hopi Buttes area, which is in the middle of the area where pure Little Colorado White Ware sites are found.

Table 5.2. *Means and standard deviations in parts per million of trace elements for gray- and sherd-tempered ceramics*

Trace element	Gray tempered			Sherd tempered			Mann–Whitney U
	Mean	Standard deviation	Sample size	Mean	Standard deviation	Sample size	
Iron	36,402	4215	21	51,946	7315	30	44[a]
Zirconium	273	18	21	258	13	30	151[b]
Strontium	281	28	21	373	72	30	106[a]
Titanium	9545	755	21	6432	1232	30	31[a]
Manganese	184	22	21	450	131	30	32[a]
Zinc	69	6	21	75	3	30	119[a]
Ribidium	202	9	21	217	11	30	91[a]

[a]Statistically significant at the 0.001 level.
[b]Statistically significant at the 0.002 level.

This association of volcanic deposits and pure Little Colorado White Ware sites suggests that the Little Colorado White Ware sherds from the Purcell–Larson area with inclusions of igneous rock fragments may have been made in the area north and northeast of Winslow. In order to compare the SShO sherds from Purcell–Larson with SShO sherds from other areas, three sherds from sites in each of three areas were thin sectioned. The sherds were from sites in the Hopi Buttes area collected by Gumerman (1969), sites in the Flagstaff area recorded by the Museum of Northern Arizona, and sites a few kilometers south of Winslow discovered by CARP. Sherds from the two former areas were supplied by the Museum of Northern Arizona. Analysis of the small sample of thin sections indicated that the sherds from immediately south of Winslow were most similar in mineral composition to the Purcell–Larson sherds (Garrett 1976).

Chemical composition
In addition to the mineral composition of PGM and SShO, other evidence must be considered. Wait (n.d.) has analyzed the chemical composition of sherd- and gray-tempered ceramics from six sites (CS numbers 118, 439, 130, 900, 734, and 503) in the Purcell–Larson area. It should be emphasized that these sherds did not have any paint on them, so it is not possible to definitely state that they were SShO and PGM sherds. However, approximately 95 percent of the sherds with gray and sherd temper that are painted have mineral and organic paint, respectively. It is therefore likely that most of the sherds analyzed by Wait were SShO and PGM sherds.

Element frequencies (in parts per million) for iron, zirconium, strontium, titanium, manganese, zinc, and rubidium were determined by Wait. He describes the method of analysis as follows:

> Selected sherd samples were analyzed with atomic absorption and colormetric methods for their major elemental components. X-ray fluorescence intensities were calibrated to these results using a General Electric XRD-700 X-ray fluorescence spectrography ... An Lif crystal, collimator with 50 kV white tungsten source and 32 mA current was utilized with an air path for all elements but Ti, Mn, and Zn. A helium path was used for the determination of these three elements. X-ray counts were recorded for both the peak analytical line intensity and the background values on either side of the peak. Since differences in elemental composition will effect the plot of intensity vs concentration, Mass Absorption Coefficients were calculated for each minor element analyzed, measuring each sherd class against a USGA G-2 standard at the appropriate wavelength. A correction based on scattered background intensities was employed for Fe and Ti ... [Wait n.d.].

Means and standard deviations were calculated for each element for the gray- and sherd-tempered ceramics for which there was no question of temper type. These are listed in Table 5.2. A Mann–Whitney test was used for each element to test the null hypothesis that the element frequencies for both classes of pottery are random samples from the same population. The values of U for each element are also shown in Table 5.2. The means and standard deviations show that the element frequencies are very different for the two pottery classes. The values of U indicate that the differences are significant at less than the 0.01 level. There is, thus, less than one chance in one hundred that the observed differences in element frequencies are a result of chance alone.

This analysis of the chemical composition of sherd- and gray-tempered ceramics supports the proposal that the two classes of pottery, PGM and SShO, were not made with clay and temper from the same source. The proposal is, thus, consistent with the mineralogical analysis.

The design analysis
As noted in Chapter 4, analysis of both SShO and PGM designs was done in order to determine whether or not there are stylistic differences between the pottery classes. This analysis revealed statistically significant differences in several design attributes. Examination of

rim sherds from 22 sites in the Purcell–Larson area showed that 40.8 percent and 49.7 percent of PGM bowl and jar rims, respectively, are decorated. In contrast, 2.1 percent and 7.4 percent of SShO bowls and jars, respectively, are decorated. A difference in proportion test (Dixon and Massey 1969:249) shows that the difference between SShO and PGM for both bowls and jars is significant at the 0.001 level.

Additional tests were carried out using the attribute frequencies for the five sites for which body sherds were analyzed. For the tests involving these attributes, the SShO attribute frequencies for each of the five sites were compared with the PGM attribute frequencies from each of the sites using a Mann–Whitney test. These tests are, thus, more stringent than the test involving rim decoration. If a test demonstrates that the attribute frequencies are significantly different, then this indicates that not only are the SShO and PGM sherds from each individual site different but also that the SShO sherds at all five sites tend to be different from the PGM sherds at all the other sites. These tests were run for all the attributes discussed in Chapter 4 and the results are shown in Table 5.3.

For primary design forms, the major difference between SShO and PGM appeared to be in the relative frequencies of triangles and terraces. Terraces were more common on PGM vessels than on SShO vessels. The Mann–Whitney tests show that this difference between the percentage of terraces (of terraces plus triangles only) is statistically significant for bowls. Statistically significant differences in the frequencies of other attribute states are also demonstrated. SShO bowls have significantly higher frequencies than PGM bowls of sherds with cross-hatching as opposed to other types of hatching. SShO jars have significantly lower frequencies than PGM jars of sherds with both hatched and solid designs, as opposed to only hatched or only solid designs, and significantly higher frequencies of appended secondary forms. Finally, SShO jars and bowls have significantly wider hatching lines, framing lines, and primary lines and a significantly greater amount of spacing between hatched lines than PGM bowls and jars.

In summary, of the 26 tests of differences between PGM and SShO, 13 are statistically significant at the 0.10 level. Of the 13 attributes measured, significant differences are demonstrated for at least one vessel form for 9 of the attributes. The tests, thus, demonstrate that there are differences between SShO and PGM in several design attributes.

Interpretation

The discussion has demonstrated that the PGM and SShO ceramic classes are different in mineral and chemical composition and in

Table 5.3. *Values of Mann–Whitney U and significance levels for comparison of design attribute frequencies for PGM and SShO bowls and jars*

Attribute	Bowls			Jars		
	Sample size	U	Sig. level	Sample size	U	Sig. level
Primary forms, percentage of terraces	(5,5)	18.0	0.056	(5,5)	20.0	0.150
Secondary forms, percentage of sherds with appended forms	(5,5)	19.5	0.124	(5,5)	15.0	0.004
Secondary forms, percentage of sherds with unappended forms	(5,5)	26.0	0.841	(5,5)	24.0	0.548
Composition, percentage of sherds with solid and hatched design	(5,5)	21.0	0.222	(5,5)	15.0	0.004
Linearity of simple lines, percentage curvilinear	(5,5)	20.0	0.150	(5,5)	23.5	0.484
Type of hatch, percentage of cross hatching	(5,5)	16.5	0.025	(4,5)	15.0	0.286
Line shape, percentage of straight line	(5,5)	27.0	1.000	(5,5)	25.0	0.690
Line interaction, percentage of parallel	(5,5)	27.0	1.000	(5,5)	26.0	0.842
Hatching line, width	(3,5)	20.0	0.072	(3,5)	21.0	0.036
Hatch framing line, width	(3,5)	21.0	0.036	(3,5)	20.5	0.054
Spacing of hatching lines	(3,5)	21.0	0.036	(3,5)	21.0	0.036
Primary line, width	(5,5)	15.0	0.004	(5,5)	23.0	0.420

design attributes. As noted previously, Wilson (1969) has proposed that SShO was imported into the Chevelon drainage and that PGM was made locally. This is one hypothesis that could explain the differences between the two pottery classes. Wait (n.d.) has argued that differences in chemical composition along with the tendency for SShO sherds to be primarily from bowls, whereas PGM sherds tend to be primarily from jars, suggests that potters were selecting different clays or different grades of the same clay to make different functional types of vessels. He suggests that the different clays may have been procured locally in the Purcell–Larson area. They also may have been obtained through long-distance procurement or through exchange. Thus, Wait proposes that SShO and PGM were both manufactured in the Purcell–Larson area. A third hypothesis that has been offered to explain the presence of volcanic material in plain ware sherds from the Chevelon area is that worn out basalt tools were ground up for temper (DeAtley 1973). Alternatively, the basalt inclusions may have resulted from the grinding of sherds for temper on basalt grinding tools, which have been found in the Chevelon area. These alternative hypotheses will now be discussed, beginning with Wait's proposal that the two pottery classes were functionally different.

In order to test Wait's proposal that PGM vessels are primarily jars and SShO vessels are primarily bowls, the relative proportions of the different vessel forms made from each pottery class must be examined. Using the body sherds from the sites included in the design study, 56 and 44 percent of the SShO sherds were bowls and jars, respectively, while 22 and 78 percent of the PGM sherds were bowls and jars, respectively. The figures support Wait's proposal. However, the test is biased because a single jar vessel "creates" more sherds when broken than a single bowl vessel. Thus, we might find more jar body *sherds* of a particular pottery class even if the number of jars and bowls made of the type in question were equal. This comparison also might be affected in a similar manner if the sizes of SShO and PGM vessels were different. The bias can be corrected and Wait's proposal retested by examining only the rim sherds of the two pottery classes. However, a comparison of the number of rim sherds would be biased somewhat also. PGM bowls from the Purcell–Larson area have an average rim circumference of 67.7 centimeters and jars have a circumference of 37.2 centimeters. For SShO, these figures are 65.0 centimeters and 43.7 centimeters, respectively. By comparing the circumferences of the two average vessels for each class, it can be seen that a bowl will "create" 1.82 times as many rim sherds as a jar for PGM vessels and 1.49 times as many rim sherds for SShO vessels if it is assumed that the sizes of the sherds from the different vessel forms are equal.

The raw counts of rim sherds from the 21 sites included in the rim design study indicate that while 93 percent of SShO vessels are bowls, 79 percent of PGM vessels are also bowls. If the bias created by the different rim circumferences of the vessel forms is corrected by multiplying the PGM jar count by 1.82 and the SShO jar count by 1.49, the majority of both SShO vessels (89 percent) and PGM vessels (57 percent) are bowls. More jar vessels were made of the PGM class, but the primary form of both pottery classes was bowls. These data do not support Wait's proposal that different types of clay or different types of temper were used to manufacture different vessel forms.

A second weakness in Wait's hypothesis and the primary weakness in the other alternative hypotheses, with the exception of vessel exchange, is that they do not explain all of the differences between SShO and PGM. These hypotheses can explain the differences in chemical and mineral composition, but they do not explain the stylistic differences between the two pottery classes. For example, if the raw materials necessary for making SShO vessels were imported, rather than the vessels themselves, and the raw materials for PGM vessels were gathered locally, there is no reason to expect stylistic differences between the classes. The hypothesis assumes that both pottery classes were made by the same group of people, and it thus would be expected that they would be decorated with the same type of paint and with the same designs. Such is not the case.

Wilson's hypothesis that SShO and PGM were not manufactured in the same areas explains all these differences. The two classes are different in chemical composition and in the relative frequencies of minerals because they were made from clays from different areas. The two classes were decorated with different types of paint and were decorated in different ways because they were manufactured and painted by different groups of people. The paste of SShO pottery is darker, suggesting it may be highly carbonaceous, because a large part of the area north of the Little Colorado River, including the area of pure SShO or Little Colorado White Ware sites, "is characterized by extensive Cretaceous formations" many of which "are highly carbonaceous" (Shepard 1953:187) and require a longer period for oxidation than alluvial and primary clays. These Cretaceous formations are absent in most parts of the Mogollon area where the principal clay sources are alluvial clays, which are low in carbonaceous material (Shepard 1953:187). Finally, the spatial distributions of PGM and SShO overlap very little. This also supports the hypothesis that they were not made in the same area.

The trade hypothesis also helps explain the change in the relative frequency of SShO through time. As noted, SShO increased through time relative to PSO, became the dominant black-on-white class about A.D. 1100, and then decreased in frequency. After A.D. 1200 it made up a small percentage of the black-on-white pottery from Chevelon sites. The appearance and increase in the relative frequency of SShO through time correlates with its appearance and increase in the Central Little Colorado River Valley. Prior to A.D. 1075, Tusayan White Ware (PSO) was the primary black-on-white pottery found in the Central Little Colorado River Valley (Gumerman and Skinner 1968:189). It was also the dominant black-on-white class in the Chevelon drainage. Other than the one known sherd of St. Joseph's Black-on-white (H. S. Colton 1955), there is no evidence that Little Colorado White Ware (SShO) was manufactured anywhere in the Southwest prior to A.D. 1025 to 1050. After this date, it became the dominant white ware in the Central Little Colorado River Valley (Gumerman and Skinner 1968:187) and in Chevelon. The increase of SShO in Chevelon is thus correlated with the beginning of its manufacture in the Central Little Colorado River Valley.

SShO continued to be the dominant black-on-white ware in the Central Little Colorado River Valley up to the time the area was abandoned by prehistoric populations. This abandonment of most of the area occurred during the latter part of the McDonald phase, dating from A.D. 1100 to 1250 (Gumerman and Skinner 1968:195). This abandonment correlates temporally with the decrease in the relative frequency of SShO in the Chevelon area. The decrease in the frequency of SShO in Chevelon then can be explained by the sharp decline in the population of the supply area. The variability in the relative frequency of SShO through time in Chevelon can thus be accounted for by events that occurred in the hypothesized supply area, the Central Little Colorado River Valley.

Conclusions
The evidence indicates that PGM and SShO were not manufactured in the same area. It *does not* demonstrate where the classes were made, but the distributions of these two classes prehistorically suggests that SShO was manufactured in the area just north of the Little Colorado River and that PGM was made in the Chevelon drainage or in the area to the east or south of Chevelon. However, the area to the south is unlikely because the Mogollon Rim separates Chevelon from this area. Thus, it is probable that SShO was not made in the Purcell–Larson area. Whether or not PGM was manufactured there or to the east remains unanswered. The available evidence neither confirms nor refutes a hypothesis of local manufacture for PGM. In addition, these data indicate that Snowflake Black-on-white, Hay Hollow variety (Longacre 1964b), was not manufactured in the Hay Hollow Valley. Although the Hay Hollow Valley does have volcanic deposits, an argument that Snowflake Black-on-white, Hay Hollow variety, was made there suffers from the same weaknesses as Wait's hypothesis of local manufacture of SShO in the Purcell–Larson area. It does not explain the design differences that exist between Hay Hollow variety and the other varieties of Snowflake Black-on-white (Longacre 1964b) or the use of organic paint on Hay Hollow variety vessels as opposed to mineral paint on the vessels of the other varieties. The Hay Hollow variety sherds are very similar in mineral composition to SShO sherds from the Purcell–Larson area (Garrett 1976). Thus, at least some of the pottery included in Longacre's analysis of designs from the Carter Ranch Site was not made at the site.

Evidence suggests that other pottery classes found on Chevelon sites may also have been imported. Design attributes of PSO and other attributes such as the presence of a carbon streak are similar to characteristics of Tusayan White Ware types of the same period from areas of northern Arizona. There are also design differences between PSO and PGM sherds. For example, only 6 percent of a small sample of 31 PSO rim sherds from the Purcell–Larson area are decorated. Thus, PSO may also have been imported into the Chevelon area. Wilson (1969:298) has suggested that this was the case for all of his localities. However, no stylistic or petrographic analyses have been done to test this hypothesis.

What this evidence indicates in regard to design variation in the Purcell–Larson area is, very simply, that a large portion of the variation in ceramic designs is a result of ceramic exchange. SShO pottery averages 81 percent of all black-on-white pottery during one time period in Chevelon. This percentage is lower during other periods, but a significant proportion and a significant total number of vessels are still being imported into the area during other periods. For example, although SShO makes up only 9 percent of the black-on-white pottery at CS 503, stylistic analysis of the rim sherds indicates that over fifty different SShO vessels are represented in the surface collection from this one site. The number of SShO vessels that were imported into the Purcell–Larson area alone during any one time period must have been in the *thousands*. The reasons this exchange system developed will be discussed in Chapter 8.

The demonstration of frequent ceramic exchange in the Chevelon area along with the results of previous studies of ceramic exchange in the American Southwest, discussed earlier, demonstrate the necessity of considering exchange and specialization in ceramic production when attempting to explain design variation. The initiation or growth of exchange systems that include ceramic vessels as one of the items traded may explain some of the temporal patterns in design variation that have been discovered in some studies, patterns that frequently have been interpreted as the result of changes in the intensity or type of social interaction and the consequent changes in design diffusion. Redman (1978:185), for example, has noted a pattern of increased design standardization through time during the last part of the thirteenth century in the Cibola area. Although he considered increased specialization in ceramic production as one possible cause of the change, that explanation was rejected. He argued (1978:185) that

> If a situation of specialized potters had emerged at CS 139, one would expect to find increasing skill of execution in technical aspects of the design. According to the values of mean line width and mean line frequency for painted

designs, the opposite pattern exists. Individual line widths are greater at CS 139 and drawn farther apart. On the basis of these measurements and qualitative impressions from complete vessels, technical competence in drawing is significantly higher at the Scribe S site.

Redman (1978:185, 190) therefore concludes that the increased design standardization was the result of an increased intensity of interaction among pottery-producing social segments. However, no mineralogical or chemical analyses were carried out to test the specialization hypothesis in a more reasonable manner. It also is not explained why line widths and distances between lines are in any way relevant measures of technical competence, nor is any evidence presented to show that increased specialization in vessel production usually results in "increasing skill of execution in technical aspects of the design." Balfet (1965) in fact has reported the opposite to be the case in one instance. She notes (1965:168) that in the Maghreb region of North Africa those who produce pottery only for their own use take special care with "minute details," while ceramic craft specialists in the area "never take the time to work in detail on the surface finish or decoration." In addition, the decreased variation in ceramics that Redman found in the Cibola area and that others (Braun 1977, Leone 1968, Whallon 1968) have noted during some time periods in different regions has been shown in one location to be a result of increased specialization in production. In the Mailu area of Papua New Guinea, Irwin (1978) used optical mineralogy and X-ray fluorescence analysis to document a reduction in the number of villages manufacturing ceramics in the area during a time period when stylistic homogeneity was increasing rapidly.

Thus, the exchange of ceramic vessels may be an important fact in explaining ceramic variation not only in the Chevelon area but also in other regions. To assume that the ceramics used in a household were manufactured in that household or that the ceramics used at a site were manufactured by the occupants of that site is not a weak or minor assumption, as Kintigh (1979:25) has argued, but is a critical, major assumption. Design analysts should neither assume local manufacture *nor* assume nonlocal production, but rather should test such hypotheses using mineralogical and chemical analysis.

6

Subsistence-settlement systems and vessel form

In Chapter 3, it was proposed that the numerous small sites in the Purcell–Larson area might be seasonal farming villages used primarily for agricultural activities. The primary reasons for suggesting this hypothesis are the small size (in terms of the number of rooms) of Purcell–Larson sites relative to some nearby areas, such as the Hay Hollow Valley area of east-central Arizona, and the low densities and low total amounts of lithics and ceramics on these sites.

A comparative study of settlement data from Hay Hollow Valley and from the southern block survey in the Purcell–Larson area by F. Plog (1974) has illustrated the differences in site size and site density between these two areas. During the periods between A.D. 1125 to 1200 and A.D. 1200 to 1275, the Purcell–Larson area had an average number of rooms per site of 2.0 and 3.0, and the percentages of all rooms occurring on sites with five or more rooms were 38 percent and 46 percent, respectively. During these same periods, the Hay Hollow Valley had an average number of rooms per site of 22.0 and 14.5, respectively, and the percentage of all rooms occurring on sites with five or more rooms was 100 percent during both periods (F. Plog 1974: Tables 3 and 4). However, site density was much higher in the Purcell–Larson area, resulting in approximately equal frequencies of rooms per square mile in the two areas during the period from A.D. 1125 to 1200 and a higher density in the Purcell–Larson area during the period from A.D. 1200 to 1275.

Comparative data on lithic and sherd densities are scarce because they are not variables that have been measured often in the Southwest. The only area with which Purcell–Larson can be compared is the extreme northern part of Black Mesa in northeastern Arizona, where a systematic unaligned sample of site surfaces was collected for over 750 sites in a 50-square mile area during 1975. Sites from this area have an average sherd density of 1.6 per square meter, and the 20 Purcell–Larson sites that were sampled to obtain artifact densities had an average ceramic density of 2.1 per square meter. However, the Purcell–Larson sites collected were chosen on the basis of their high artifact densities. Thus, they should have higher sherd densities than the average Purcell–Larson site. For a more valid comparison, the artifact density on the Black Mesa sites that are above the population median can be calculated. The average ceramic density on these sites is approximately 3.0 sherds per square meter. Artifact density in the Purcell–Larson area is thus similar to Black Mesa.

Sites such as those in the Purcell–Larson area that have few rooms and low artifact densities have often been interpreted as seasonal farming villages, particularly in areas in which larger sites are also frequent (Bradley 1959; Gregory 1975). However, there are few large sites spatially associated with the small sites in the Purcell–Larson area. The largest site in this area has 16 rooms (CS 690), the next largest has 10 rooms (CS 616 and CS 522), and there are only a few other sites that have more than 5 rooms.

In order to determine whether or not the numerous small Purcell–Larson sites are seasonal farming villages, at least two questions must be answered. First, are the Purcell–Larson sites different in size from sites in surrounding areas where the populations farming in the Purcell–Larson area may have resided most of the year? If sites in the surrounding areas are no larger than the Purcell–Larson sites, the hypothesis that Purcell–Larson sites were seasonal farming villages would not be supported because one of the reasons for initially suggesting that they were seasonal villages was that they were small. If all sites over a broad area are also small, however, this reasoning becomes less plausible. Second, are the artifact assemblages of Purcell–Larson sites and sites in surrounding areas functionally different? If they are not, then the hypothesis that Purcell–Larson sites are seasonal farming villages would not be supported. Even though these are not the only questions that are relevant to determining the seasonality of sites in the area, they are the only ones that can be answered with the data currently available. Each of these questions will now be considered.

Site size
The entire Chevelon drainage was sampled by CARP during 1971. This survey covers a broad area and provides a data base for comparison with the Purcell–Larson area. The average size of sites with rooms in the Chevelon drainage is 3.5, as noted previously. (All sites located by the 1971 survey were included when calculating this average.) Other than Chevelon Ruin, which postdates all of the Purcell–Larson sites, the largest site in the drainage is CS 203, which lies just 1 kilometer east of the Purcell–Larson area. This site has between 45 and 69 rooms, but consists of several spatially separate room blocks whose contemporaneity are not known. Only two other sites with

Table 6.1. *Frequency table of number of rooms per site for four areas in east-central Arizona*

Rooms per site	Chevelon drainage	Pinedale	Clear Creek	Purcell–Larson
1	33	9	7	23
2	20	4	9	14
3	14	2	8	12
4	5	0	1	6
5	4	0	4	1
6–10	8	2	3	4
11–20	1	0	1	2
21–30	1	0	1	0
31–50	0	0	0	0
51–75	1	1	0	0
Means	3.53	6.22	3.76	2.87

more than 10 rooms were located by the 1971 survey. Large sites are thus infrequent throughout the drainage. A frequency table of the number of rooms on sites with structures for the Chevelon drainage as a whole and for a systematic random sample of the Purcell–Larson area is presented in Table 6.1, along with the average number of rooms for such sites. The frequency table shows that the average size of sites with rooms in the Chevelon drainage and in Purcell–Larson are highly similar. The average size of sites within the Chevelon drainage as a whole is only slightly higher than in the Purcell–Larson area, and the frequency of large sites is approximately equal. In addition, comparison of lithic and ceramic assemblages collected from the surfaces of sites of different sizes within the drainage, including the Purcell–Larson area, has suggested that there is no consistent relationship between the tool assemblage of a site and its size as measured by the number of structures (McAllister and Plog 1978). Thus, throughout the drainage, different activities do not appear to have been carried out at large versus small sites.

The survey of Wilson (1969) along Clear Creek to the west of Chevelon drainage provides an additional area with which Purcell–Larson can be compared. If we use those sites for which clear estimates of the number of rooms are provided, we find that the average number of rooms for the sites with structures located by Wilson was 3.8 rooms per site, and the largest of the 34 sites had a minimum of 15 rooms (Wilson 1969: Table 7). A frequency table of site sizes for the Clear Creek survey also is presented in Table 6.1. Again, the average size of sites and the frequency of large sites are similar to the Purcell–Larson area. In addition, Wilson (1969:311) noted that different types of brown ware were found in the Clear

Creek and Heber areas, which suggests that the same population was not inhabiting both areas. Thus, neither the data on site size nor the stylistic information on ceramics from the Clear Creek area suggest that the area was the locus of permanent habitation sites occupied by populations who farmed seasonally in the Purcell–Larson area.

Available information on site size from the Chevelon drainage and Clear Creek drainage does not support the hypothesis that Purcell–Larson sites are seasonal farming villages. However, limited data from the area east and southeast of Purcell–Larson suggested prior to this study that the former area might be a region where the average size of sites with rooms might be significantly higher than in the Purcell–Larson area. Pinedale and Bailey Ruins, each of which probably consisted of about two hundred rooms, had previously been sampled by Haury (Haury and Hargrave 1931). However, no survey work had been done in the area, so it was not known how common such large sites were in Pinedale; it was, in part, for this reason that the area was surveyed by CARP during the summer of 1974.

A frequency table of site size was constructed for the Pinedale area, using the sites located by the transect survey and the Day Burn block survey during 1974, and is presented in Table 6.1 along with the frequency table for the Purcell–Larson area. The transect survey and the Day Burn block survey include the only areas where survey locations were not purposefully located where large sites were known to be present. Thus, they should provide the most representative estimate of the frequency in the Pinedale region of sites of different sizes. Mean site size for sites with rooms in Pinedale is higher, with 6.2 rooms per site, than in Purcell–Larson. However, this increase is primarily a consequence of the discovery of one pueblo (CS 936) with an estimated seventy-five rooms during the transect survey. Without this one site, the average rooms per site in Pinedale would be 2.2, actually lower than Purcell–Larson. Without any knowledge of the area other than the random sample of transects, it could be predicted that there are approximately one hundred sites as large as CS 936 in Pinedale, because the probability sample covered less than 1 percent of the area. If this were true, it would support the proposal that the Purcell–Larson sites are seasonal villages occupied by populations from many large, permanent communities in the Pinedale area.

However, I would suggest that there are several reasons why large pueblos are not as frequent in Pinedale as would be expected. First, it has been shown that the percentage of the total number of sites in a sample universe that are found using a probability sample is greater than the percentage of the land area surveyed. With a survey of 1 percent of area, more than 1 percent of the sites in that area will be found (S. Plog, F. Plog, and Wait 1978: 396–8). Given the results of previous experiments (S. Plog, F. Plog, and Wait 1978: 396) and a sampling fraction of less than 1 percent for the Pinedale survey, it would be expected that the actual number of sites in the entire region would be about one-half of the total number that would be estimated from the sample. Second, experiments have shown that the larger sites in an area have a greater probability of being discovered in a sample (S. Plog, F. Plog, and Wait 1978:400). As a result, estimates of the frequency of large sites may be inflated. Finally, all but one of the large pueblos that were located in the area, including the only one located by the random sample (CS 936), were known by local amateurs and Forest Service personnel. These sites were found by talking with these individuals and then surveying the general areas where they stated the sites were located. The detailed knowledge of the area by local amateurs, the fact that the survey work located only one large site which these individuals had not mentioned, and the inflated estimates of total sites and particularly large sites that result from surveys with low sampling fractions – all taken into consideration – prompt the suggestion that the large pueblos of which we have knowledge constitute at least a 75 percent sample of all such sites and possibly a 90 to 100 percent sample. If this is true, it would mean that large sites in the Pinedale area are less frequent than the random sample estimate indicates. The existence of only four to six large pueblos in the Pinedale area would not support the hypothesis that Purcell–Larson sites are seasonal villages occupied by large, permanent communities in the Pinedale area. It is unlikely that the population of a few such pueblos was large enough to have constructed the thousands of small sites in the Purcell–Larson area unless the occupation length of the small sites was much shorter than the occupation length of the large sites. In addition, there are numerous small pueblos in the Pinedale area itself that could be field houses used by the populations of the large communities.

To summarize, I propose that the data on site size indicate that the Purcell–Larson area is similar in site size to nearby areas where research has been done. It is possible that populations moved seasonally into the Purcell–Larson region from areas more distant than those already discussed. Areas such as the Hay Hollow Valley to the east or the Grasshopper region 45 to 50 kilometers (28 to 31 miles) south of the Purcell–Larson region, for example, are known to have had numerous large communities during the time the Purcell–Larson area was occupied. However, although seasonal movements over such distances may have been possible, there is no data to support the occurrence of such movements. Also, Lipe (1970:120) has noted a number of logistical problems that would be created by moves over such distances. It is thus unlikely that all sites in the Purcell–Larson area were seasonal farming villages used by populations who resided more permanently in other areas. In addition, to argue on the basis of site size alone that Purcell–Larson sites were seasonally occupied would mean that almost 90 percent of the known sites with surface structures in the area between Silver Creek near the Hay Hollow Valley (see Figure 5.1) and Clear Creek, an area about 60 kilometers (37 miles) wide, would have to be interpreted in the same way.

The increased amount of archaeological work in the American Southwest in "marginal" areas away from the better known regions such as Chaco Canyon and Mesa Verde almost always has resulted in one common conclusion: small sites are much more common than previously thought and actually make up 80 to 100 percent of the pueblo sites found (F. Plog, Effland, and Green 1978). Examples supporting this statement – in addition to the Chevelon, Pinedale, and Clear Creek areas – are the Black Mesa area of northeastern Arizona (Gumerman, Westfall, and Weed 1972), the Hopi Buttes area of north central Arizona (Gumerman 1969), the Glen Canyon area of southern Utah and northern Arizona (Jennings 1966), and the Red Rock Plateau area of southern Utah (Lipe 1970). Inevitably, the question of whether or not these small sites were seasonal has arisen, and it has been concluded that they were not (Gumerman 1969, 1970; Gumerman, Westfall, and Weed 1972; Jennings 1966:63). It has become clear that small sites that were originally thought to be atypical are, in fact, typical. Our knowledge of Southwestern prehistory had been skewed either by the amount of research in atypical areas such as Mesa Verde or on the larger, more spectacular sites in other areas.

Site assemblages

In addition to simply comparing the sizes of sites, a more direct method of determining whether or not the Purcell–Larson sites were seasonal farming villages is to determine if artifact assemblages are functionally different from sites in surrounding areas. As noted, if the assemblages are not different, then the hypothesis that Purcell–Larson sites were seasonal farming villages would not be supported.

Unfortunately, little excavation has been done in surrounding areas, so a comparative study of entire assemblages cannot be made. Only data collected from site surfaces during the Pinedale survey are available. A problem arises in using these surface collections because the types of artifacts that previously have been the focus of functional analyses, lithics and ground stone, are not abundant on the surfaces of sites in the Chevelon and Pinedale areas. Only samples of ceramics are large enough for meaningful comparisons between sites. However, most ceramic studies in the American Southwest have focused on stylistic attributes, while little attention has been given to functional aspects of pottery. In many previous reports, inferences have been made concerning the functions of different ceramic types and descriptions have been given of vessel forms, but functional analysis normally has ended with these simple types of statements.

Recently, however, it has been argued that ceramic assemblages should be regarded as tools just as lithics or ground stone are (Binford 1965:206; Ericson, Read, and Burke 1972; Braun 1974). From this perspective, data concerning intrasite and intersite variation in ceramic assemblages are an important source of information concerning the types of activities that took place in prehistoric communities. Given the abundance of ceramics on the surface of most archaeological sites in the American Southwest such as the Purcell–Larson area and the absence of ecofactual data for unexcavated sites, functional ceramic analyses could potentially provide useful information concerning prehistoric activities. However, before such analyses can provide such information, we must have some basis for drawing inferences concerning vessel functions from various attributes of the pottery. In the sections that follow, I will discuss some attributes which, on the basis of ethnographic evidence and archaeological data, seem to be useful for functional analysis.

Decoration

It is often assumed by archaeologists in the American Southwest and elsewhere that corrugated (and plain ware) vessels were culinary wares and painted vessels were used for nonculinary purposes such as the serving of food and the storage of food and water. If this division is reliable, it would be useful in the study of site functions. Intersite variation in the relative frequencies of these vessel types would be indicative of variation in the relative frequency of activities such as food preparation and food storage. For example, it might be suggested that a site with a relatively small percentage of painted wares would indicate a site where food was processed but not stored or consumed. At other types of sites, such as habitation sites, the ceramic assemblage should include vessels for serving and storing food as well as food processing. However, the validity of this assumption must be considered first; in that regard, some relevant ethnographic data will be presented.

Studies of the ceramic assemblages of contemporary native American groups in the American Southwest suggest that those people do not paint cooking vessels. The reason for this seems to be that the use of a painted vessel over a fire would result in carbon deposits obscuring the design. Statements concerning the uses of painted and unpainted vessels were found for several groups:

[Navajo] cooking ware is said never to have been painted [Tschopik 1941:8].

A [Papago] potter sees no need to decorate a pot that is going to be placed over an open fire and thus have its design obliterated. This does not mean, however, that painted pots are never used for cooking [Fontana et al. 1962:49].

Decorations were never applied to [Kamia] culinary wares, but all other wares were occasionally decorated with geometrical designs [Rogers 1936:26].

Except for [Mohave] vessels like cook pots and parchers, where decoration would be wasted, painting is the rule, and mostly, painting on both sides [Kroeber and Harner 1955:10].

Cooking ware and any other types made for hard usage [by the Yuma] are not painted; water and food-storage wares are the ones most often decorated [Rogers 1936:32].

A great part of the Pima ceramic ware is plain and un-decorated. The cooling ollas in which water is kept about their homes are the only vessels that are generally deco-rated [Russell 1975:124].

Decoration was not applied to [Maricopa] cooking pots and parching pans since these were soon blackened in use. Water jars were painted red over the exterior, ladles in their entirety. Bowls or cups were solid or white inside and out, with designs in black [Spier 1970:106].

In addition, a similar pattern has been reported for pottery-making groups in other areas of the world such as the Aymara, Shipibo, and Conibo of Peru (Tschopik 1950:206–8; Myers 1975:340).

It should be noted that exceptions to the rule are mentioned for two of these groups, the Papago and the Navaho (Fontana et al. 1962:49; Tschopik 1941:10). No statements concerning other groups have yet been found that contradict the above statements. Although reports on the ceramics of Southwestern groups other than those listed here are available, it is either not stated that all vessels were painted or the functions of the painted and unpainted vessels are not discussed. While these could be viewed as indications that all vessels of these groups are painted or that there are no functional differences between painted and unpainted vessels, I feel they should not be interpreted in this way. Simply because the eth-nographer does not state that there are functional differences be-tween unpainted and painted vessels does not mean that these func-tional differences did not exist. For example, Roger's (1936:36–7) discussion of Mohave pottery does not indicate whether or not all vessels are painted. However, the previous quote from Krober and Harners' report does state that all Mohave vessels are not painted and that only certain functional classes of vessels are so treated.

The ethnographic evidence thus indicates two points: (1) painted vessels are not used for cooking, and (2) some, but not necessarily all, unpainted vessels were used for cooking.

Vessel Form

A second attribute on which functional studies of ceramic vessels can be based is vessel form. A relationship between form and function has long been postulated by archaeologists (Roberts 1929:207) and some authors of ethnographic studies on pottery making have made similar statements concerning the products of the people whom they studied (Fontana et al. 1962:133; Thompson 1958:27, 146). Recently, Braun (1974) has made an intensive study of ethnographic descriptions of ceramic assemblages for Southwestern groups and the functions that are listed for the different vessel forms. On the basis of this study, Braun (1974:1) suggested that particular vessel forms tended to be used for particular types of activities in all the groups whose assemblages he studied.

More specifically, Braun has argued that "domestic activities involving the use of ceramic containers were found to be differentiable in terms of the different frequencies of access and degrees of containment security they involved" (1974:1). He states that those aspects of vessel form that seemed to covary with differences among activities in access frequency and containment security are the size of the vessel orifice and the presence or absence of a zone of restriction at the vessel mouth (1974:2). For example, vessels used for activities requiring secure containment but a low access frequency, such as storage, would have a small, restricted mouth while pots used in an activity such as food consumption where the need for security is low and the access frequency is high would have a wide, unrestricted mouth (Braun 1974:2). Given this association between particular activities and the shape and size of vessel mouths, Braun suggests that it is possible to obtain information on the activities performed at sites through the analysis of rim sherds (1974:3).

Braun's research was based on descriptions of ceramic assemblages for the Papago, Yuman groups, Pima, and Stevenson's Pueblo ceramic collections. The association between mouth shape and size and vessel function also seems to hold for the Navaho (Tschopik 1941), Yucatecan Maya (Thompson 1958) and the Aymara of Peru (Tschopik 1950), groups which were not included in the sample on which Braun's study was based. Vessel form, then, is a second attribute on which inferences concerning vessel function can be made.

Raw Materials and their physical properties

A final attribute that may be useful in isolating vessel function is the type of material used in constructing the vessels. Shepard (1971), Matson (1965), DeAtley (1973), and Ericson, Read, and Burke (1972:86) have all suggested that there is a relationship between raw materials and the manner in which the finished vessels are used. DeAtley (1973:11) has noted that there are two assumptions underlying this proposition:

> First, . . . different materials have different properties because of their varying compositions. These properties determine the physical properties that a finished ceramic will have, technology being held constant, and the kind of manipulation and treatment they will require in order to make pottery with that technology. Next, in order to use pottery effectively for certain functions, or sets of tasks, it must have sets of specifiable physical properties suited to those uses [Ericson, Read, and Burke 1972:86]. Because it is the combinations of raw materials which yield the physical properties of the ceramic material, primary functions of pottery dictate the kinds of materials which must be selected under any given technology to obtain the desired properties.

If this proposition is true, there should be ethnographic evidence that people choose different clays or different tempering materials for vessels used for different purposes. The ethnographic data for the American Southwest indicate that not all societies use different types of temper for different functional types of vessels. The Navajo (Tschopik 1941:18) and Maricopa (Spier 1970) are both reported to use only one type of temper. However, there is also evidence that potters in a number of societies do use different tempers or clays for different types of vessels. Fontana and others (1962) report that Papago potters generally use only one kind of temper, but note that one potter said that a coarse temper is used to make vessels more porous and thus better evaporators and coolers (1962:34, 57). San Ildefonso (Guthe 1925:22), Pima (Russell 1975:124–5), and Diegueno (Rogers 1936:4) potters use particular clay sources to make cooking vessels. Rogers (1936:31, 37) reports that the Yuma and Mohave use sherd temper for all vessels except cooking wares. The Yuma use granite temper in cooking vessels, and the Mohave use sandstone temper. The Hopi use the same clay source for making all types of vessels but add sandstone temper for cooking and storage vessels; no temper is added to the clay when making other types of vessels (M. Colton 1938:7).

In Mesoamerica, Thompson (1958:36–69, 71) reports that the Yucatecan Maya have a tendency to use limestone temper for making water vessels and calcite temper for cooking vessels. Thompson reports that the Mayan potters feel that the calcite-tempered vessels withstand heat better than the limestone tempered vessels (1958:113). Arnold (1971) studied the raw materials used by potters in the Mayan community of Ticul. Analysis by X-ray diffraction showed that the temper called *sah kab*, which Thompson reports as limestone, consisted of attapulgite as a clay mineral component and calcite and dolomite as nonclay mineral components, while the temper called *hi'*, which Thompson reported as calcite temper, consisted of microcrystalline calcites as a nonclay mineral component with clay mineral components absent (Arnold 1971:32–4). Arnold also reports that *sah kab* temper was used in making all pottery not used for cooking, while *hi'* temper was used for making cooking pottery (1971:32–3). Finally, the Chontal in Tabasco, Mexico, use fine sand in making water vessels and coarse sand in making cooking pots (Thompson 1958:145).

This evidence does suggest that different raw materials may be used for functionally different types of vessels and hence supports the proposition that there is relationship between raw materials and the uses of vessels. However, if the proposition is correct, it would also be expected that the types of tempers or clays used for different functional types of vessels should have properties suited to the uses of the vessels, as DeAtley has suggested in the previous quote. For example, DeAtley (1973:39) has argued that raw materials promoting high levels of vessel porosity would be expected to be used in cooking vessels. A vessel's resistance to thermal shock, which would be expected to be high for cooking vessels (Ericson, Read, and Burke 1972:89), varies directly with porosity (Shepard 1971:126).

Given this expectation, we can ask whether there is any evidence that the types of tempers used ethnographically would have physical properties similar to those predicted. In this regard, it can first be reiterated that the ethnographic evidence shows that crushed rock temper (Yuma, Mohave, and Hopi), clay for which no temper is needed (San Ildefonso, Pima, and Diegueno), or coarse sand (Chontal) are used for cooking vessels and that sherd temper (Pima, Yuma, and Mohave), sand temper (Pima), or fine sand temper (Chontal) are used for other types of vessels. For the Pima, Russell's notes suggest that no temper needs to be added to clay used for cooking vessels because there are numerous coarse inclusions in the clay naturally. He states (1975:124–5):

> The common ware that is intended to be subjected to heat is generally made from clay obtained among the Skasowalik hills, which lie on the southern border of the Gila River reservation. The material is a dry granular clay

> combined with quartz pebbles and feldspathic detritus. The place where it occurs looks much more like a stone quarry than like a clay pit. Indeed, a great part of the mass is sharp, angular stone, which must be winnowed out by hand in the shallow baskets . . .
>
> The clay from Skasowalik hills is so coarse that it requires no tempering.

This may also be the case for the Diegueno, inasmuch as Rogers (1936:4) notes that their clay used for cooking vessels is highly micaceous.

These data suggest that coarser types of temper are used in making cooking pots. The evidence for the Hopi and Chontal provide the best support for this inference. In addition, Arnold's description of the tempering material used in Ticul are consistent with the suggested pattern. *Sah kb* temper, used for noncooking pots, "is very light in weight and becomes soft and pliable like clay when it is wet," whereas *hi'* temper is a crystalline substance (Arnold 1971:34, 35).

The use of coarse temper for cooking vessels is not unexpected given the prediction that cooking vessels should have high levels of porosity and thus high resistance to thermal shock. Porosity is directly related to the size of the particles and inversely related to the amount of variation in the size of the particles (Shepard 1971:127). No ethnographic information was found on variation in the size of temper particles, so this aspect of the argument must remain unevaluated. However, the available ethnographic evidence does suggest that potters use raw materials with particular physical properties for different functional types of vessels.

The ethnographic evidence suggests that variation in three attributes is related to vessel function. These attributes are: (1) the presence-absence of decoration, (2) vessel form, and (3) the type and coarseness of temper used. Rather than assume that variation in these attributes also was functionally determined prehistorically, relevant archaeological data must be considered in order to assess the validity of the hypothesis in regard to prehistoric ceramic assemblages. Because of the lack of functional analyses of ceramics in the American Southwest, a detailed analysis of Chevelon ceramics was carried out to test the hypothesis. This analysis will now be described.

Chevelon ceramics

In order to systematically test the postulated covariation between type of temper, vessel form, and the presence-absence of painted designs, several tests were carried out using ceramic data collected for this purpose during the summer of 1974. In addition, ceramic data collected during other summers was used when possible. The general procedure was to consider two attributes at a time, and statistically test to determine whether or not there was any relationship between the attributes. Thus, in the sections that follow each of the three possible combinations of two attributes, temper and form, temper and presence-absence of painted designs, and form and presence-absence of painted designs, will be examined in turn to determine whether or not covariation can be demonstrated.

First, however, some basic aspects of the data measurement should be described. Temper was in all cases determined by examining a fresh break on a sherd with, at minimum, a ten-power hand lens. These identifications were made by individuals who had been carefully trained to recognize the different types of temper known to exist in the Chevelon area. The sorting criteria used in making the identifications were developed by F. Plog after examination of several hundred sherds using a high-powered binocular microscope. Identifications of vessel form on painted body sherds were determined by noting whether the paint occurred on the convex or concave surface of the sherd. If the paint was on the concave surface or on both surfaces the sherd was considered a fragment of a bowl. If it was painted on the convex surface the sherd was considered a fragment of a jar. Unpainted white ware body sherds were not included in any of the analysis described here. For white ware rim sherds, form identifications were again based on which surface(s) paint was found, along with the angle of the sherd when the rim was inverted and placed on a flat surface in such a manner that all parts of the rim were in contact with the flat surface. Form judgments for unpainted rim sherds were made using the latter method only. More specific form measurements will be discussed later.

Covariation of temper and painted designs
Several types of tempering materials were used in manufacturing the pottery found in the Chevelon area. Black-on-white ceramics, as already noted, were tempered with sand or with one of two types of sherd temper. The undecorated plain and corrugated sherds were tempered with sand, crushed rock, or sherd. The ethnographic data previously presented indicated that when a group used more than one type of tempering material, noncooking vessels were tempered with crushed sherd or with a less coarse sand temper than that used in cooking vessels. Ethnographic data also indicated that cooking vessels were not painted with designs. Thus, it should be expected that prehistoric vessels with painted designs should be tempered with crushed sherd or fine sand.

The degree of covariation between type of tempering material and the presence-absence of painted designs can be tested using

Table 6.2. *Frequencies of different types of temper for deco-rated and undecorated pottery**

	Decorated		Undecorated	
	Count	Percentage	Count	Percentage
Sherd temper	3264	24.5	682	4.1
Sand temper	1062	75.5	2713	16.1
Crushed rock temper	0	0.0	13,424	79.8
Totals	4326	100.0	16,819	100.0

* χ^2 = 12,988.4, significance level = 0.01.

ceramic data collected during the 1971 survey of the Chevelon drain-age. The frequencies of different types of temper for sherds with and without painted designs are shown in Table 6.2. Seventy-five percent of the black-on-white sherds were tempered with crushed sherd, but only 4 percent of the undecorated pottery was tempered with that material. The chi-square statistic for the table is significant at the 0.01 level. These figures indicate that type of temper and the presence-ab-sence of decoration are not independent and suggest a high degree of covariation between the two attributes as predicted.

It also would be expected, given the ethnographic data, that the sand temper used in the painted wares would be finer than the sand temper used in unpainted wares. A visual inspection with a hand lens suggests this is true, but no measurements of grain size have been made to test the hypothesis.

Covariation of decoration and form
The ethnographic data also indicates that types of temper and vessel form should covary. Braun's (1974) study of vessel forms has shown ethnographically that cooking vessels were usually wide-mouthed jars with short necks and storage vessels usually had narrow orifices and high necks. Braun (1974:13) notes that bowls and platters were used for activities requiring frequent access and little containment security such as mixing, serving, and eating.

Given this information, it should be expected that unpainted vessels and painted vessels will have different vessel forms, on the average. Unpainted vessels should be primarily wide-mouthed jars because vessels with these attributes are used ethnographically to cook food. Painted vessels should be primarily bowls or narrow-mouthed jars inasmuch as vessels of this type are used for noncooking activities. To determine whether or not these expectations were met, rim sherds collected in the Purcell–Larson area during 1974 were sorted into white ware and red ware (decorated), plain ware and corrugated (un-

Table 6.3. *Frequencies of bowls and jars for plain ware, corrugated, and white and red wares*

	Bowls		Jars	
	Count	Percentage	Count	Percentage
White and red ware	1055	79.3	175	17.0
Plain ware	82	6.2	62	6.0
Corrugated	194	14.6	795	77.0
Totals	1331	100.1	1032	100.0

χ^2 = 976.4, significance level = 0.01.

decorated) categories, and the vessel form (bowl or jar) was recorded. The proportions of bowls and jars for white ware and red ware versus plain ware and corrugated sherds are shown in Table 6.3. The figures indicate that white ware and red ware rim sherds were primarily from bowls while plain ware and corrugated rim sherds were primarily from jars, as expected. A chi-square test was significant at the 0.01 level, indicating that vessel form and the presence-absence of decoration are not independent.

As argued earlier, it should also be the case that decorated versus undecorated (plain ware and corrugated) jars should have different orifice diameters. To test this hypothesis, the orifice diameters of rim sherds were measured on a chart on which concentric circles with increments of 1 centimeter in diameter were drawn. The diameter of the circle whose curvature corresponded most closely to the curvature of the sherd was used as an estimate of the orifice diameter of the vessel. All rim sherds collected from the Purcell–Larson sites during 1974 that were large enough for a reliable measurement to be made were measured in this manner. A frequency table of orifice diameters for the various vessel categories is presented in Table 6.4. The statistics for the orifice diameters of decorated (white and red ware) bowls and jars, and undecorated (plain ware and corrugated) bowls and jars are shown in Table 6.5. As expected, the average orifice diameter of decorated jars is less than that of undecorated jars, with values of 11.6 and 22.7 centimeters, respectively. A Kolmogorov–Smirnov test was used to test the null hypothesis that both samples have been drawn from identical populations. This nonparametric test was used rather than a parametric test, because the assumptions of the parametric tests, normal distributions and equal variances, could not be met either with the original values or with log transformations of these values. The test showed that the two samples were significantly different with one chance in one thousand that the difference is the result of chance alone.

Table 6.4. *Frequency table of orifice diameters (in centimeters) for PGM vessels, SShO bowls, corrugated bowls and jars, and black-on-red bowls*

Orifice diameter interval	B/R bowls	PGM bowls	SShO bowls	Corrugated bowls	PGM jars	Corrugated jars
2–3 cm	0	0	0	0	1	0
4–5	0	0	3	0	3	3
6–7	1	5	1	0	16	4
8–9	0	10	3	2	25	7
10–11	1	22	8	1	28	18
12–13	4	31	24	6	28	30
14–15	5	40	19	4	25	59
16–17	6	48	30	14	11	59
18–19	9	35	31	18	3	51
20–21	11	42	13	19	5	64
22–23	7	52	25	17	1	72
24–25	12	35	19	18	0	69
26–27	10	37	16	9	1	55
28–29	6	20	11	12	0	46
30–31	4	14	8	12	0	44
32–33	2	25	9	6	0	22
34–35	2	12	3	8	0	23
36–37	2	8	2	2	0	12
38–39	4	3	0	2	0	8
40+	6	8	5	14	0	16
Totals	92	447	230	164	147	662

The difference between the orifice diameters of decorated versus undecorated bowls also was tested using a Kolmogorov–Smirnov test. These types of bowls had average orifice diameters of 21.6 and 25.3 centimeters, respectively. Again, the tests showed that the difference is statistically significant at the 0.001 level. Thus, not only are the proportions of gross vessel forms different for vessels that are painted and unpainted but also the orifice diameters are different for jars that are painted and unpainted and the same is true for painted and unpainted bowls. As expected, painted jars had smaller orifices than did undecorated jars. Thus, all of this information suggests a high degree of covariation between vessel form and the presence-absence of painted designs.

Covariation of temper and form
Ethnographic information indicates that cooking vessels are tempered with sand or crushed rock and have the vessel form already described. Noncooking vessels have different forms and are tempered with fine sand or crushed sherd. To test whether or not

Table 6.5. *Descriptive statistics and test statistics for decorated and undecorated bowls and jars, and bowls and jars with and without sherd temper*

| | Orifice diameters | |
	Jars	Bowls
Decorated[a]		
Mean	11.6 cm	21.6 cm
Standard deviation	4.0	7.9
Sample size	171	837
Undecorated[b]		
Mean	22.7	25.3
Standard deviation	8.1	8.2
Sample size	689	186
Test statistics	$D = 0.670$	$D = 0.161$
	$D_{0.001} = 0.167$	$D_{0.001} = 0.158$

[a] White and red ware.
[b] Plain ware and corrugated.

the attributes of temper and form covary in the expected manner prehistorically in the Chevelon area, the ceramics from the Purcell–Larson area collected during 1974 again were used. Rim sherds tempered with different materials were sorted into the gross form categories mentioned. The frequencies of different forms for the temper types are shown in Table 6.6. A chi-square statistic was calculated using the frequencies shown in the table. The statistic was significant at the 0.01 level, indicating that type of temper and vessel form are not independent.

The average orifice diameters of bowls and jars tempered with different materials were also calculated. The statistics are presented in Table 6.7. The figures indicate that jars tempered with different materials have different orifice diameters as do bowls tempered with different materials. The differences were tested for statistical significance using a Kolmogorov–Smirnov test. The tests indicated that the differences between bowl orifice diameters is significant at the 0.001 level, while the difference between jar orifice diameters also is significant at the 0.001 level. Again, this supports the proposition that types of temper and vessel form vary with the function of the vessel.

Summary
The tests demonstrate that the attributes of temper, form, and presence-absence of painted designs covary in the manner expected on the basis of ethnographic data. This covariation supports the inference that vessels with different forms and temper and with and

Table 6.6. *Frequencies of bowls and jars for different temper categories*

	Bowls		Jars	
	Count	Percentage	Count	Percentage
Sherd temper	879	76.8	177	17.3
Sand temper	249	21.7	825	80.7
Crushed rock temper	17	1.5	20	2.0
Totals	1145	100.0	1022	100.0

$\chi^2 = 771.4$, significance level $= 0.01$.

Table 6.7. *Descriptive statistics and test statistics for orifice diameters of bowls and jars with and without sherd temper*

	Orifice diameters	
	Jars	Bowls
Sherd temper		
Mean	11.6 cm	21.2 cm
Standard deviation	4.0	7.8
Sample size	170.0	703.0
Nonsherd temper		
Mean	22.7	24.9
Standard deviation	8.1	8.1
Sample size	690.0	199.0
Test statistics	$D = 0.670$	$D = 0.180$
	$D_{0.001} = 0.167$	$D_{0.001} = 0.157$

without painted designs were used for different functions prehistorically. Unpainted jars have sand or crushed rock temper and wide orifices and were used for cooking. Painted jars have crushed sherd temper and narrow orifices and were used for storage. Painted bowls have crushed sherd temper and wide orifices and were used for food preparation, serving, and eating. The only frequently occurring type of vessel for which the function is uncertain is unpainted bowls with crushed rock temper and wider orifices than painted bowls. The wide orifices indicate that these vessels were not used for activities where containment security was required and thus were likely used in food preparation and serving also. While the difference between average orifice diameters of painted and unpainted bowls is statistically significant, the average difference is only 3.7 centimeters. I would argue that there is very little substantive difference between the two types of vessels. The ethnographic data discussed earlier indicate that all cooking vessels are unpainted but that all unpainted vessels are not cook-

Table 6.8. *Relative frequencies of bowls, decorated jars, and undecorated jars on Pinedale and Purcell–Larson sites*

Site number	No. of rooms	Area	Percentage bowls	Percentage decorated jars	Percentage undecorated jars
43	3–6	Purcell–Larson	51.0	7.0	42.0
409	4	Purcell–Larson	56.5	7.1	36.5
410	1	Purcell–Larson	58.0	8.0	34.0
411	1	Purcell–Larson	59.2	8.5	32.4
412	7	Purcell–Larson	45.2	11.3	43.5
439	2	Purcell–Larson	26.4	5.3	68.4
451	2	Purcell–Larson	68.1	14.9	17.0
466	2	Purcell–Larson	65.8	3.8	30.4
483	15–20	Purcell–Larson	60.4	10.4	29.2
496	7	Purcell–Larson	48.3	6.0	45.7
499	2–3	Purcell–Larson	60.3	2.1	37.6
503	3	Purcell–Larson	50.9	9.4	39.7
519	4	Purcell–Larson	65.3	10.2	24.5
522	10	Purcell–Larson	60.9	10.2	28.9
720	4–6	Purcell–Larson	62.8	5.0	32.1
734	2	Purcell–Larson	67.3	7.6	25.0
813	3	Purcell–Larson	48.9	8.5	42.6
969	15–20	Pinedale	34.8	22.7	42.4
974	2–5	Pinedale	51.6	8.3	40.0
975	30+	Pinedale	43.1	7.7	49.2
1009	8–12	Pinedale	45.0	6.0	49.0
1015	5–10	Pinedale	68.1	13.6	18.2

ing vessels. Thus, in the analysis that follows, painted and unpainted bowls will be regarded as functionally equivalent regardless of what type of material they are tempered with.

Using the three functional classes of vessels established, artifact assemblages on sites in the Purcell–Larson and Pinedale areas can now be compared to determine whether or not they are similar. The relative frequencies of decorated and undecorated bowl rims, decorated (white ware only as there are no red ware jars) jar rims, and undecorated plain ware and corrugated jar rims from five sites in the Pinedale area and seventeen sites in the Purcell–Larson areas from which large samples of rim sherds could be collected were tabulated and are shown in Table 6.8. The sites from the Pinedale area include most of the largest sites discovered in that area and are thus the most likely to be sites that were occupied year round. The average frequencies of the three functional ceramic classes are similar in the two areas. Bowls make up an average of 56 and 49 percent of the assemblages in the Purcell–Larson and Pinedale areas, respectively. Decorated jars have average relative frequencies of 8.0 percent and 11.7 percent, respectively. If the Purcell–Larson sites were seasonally occupied and the Pinedale sites were permanent habitation sites, then it would be expected that the latter group of sites would have significantly higher relative frequencies of storage vessels and significantly lower relative frequencies of cooking and serving vessels than the Purcell–Larson sites. The similarity of the assemblages from the two groups of sites was tested using a Mann–Whitney statistic. These tests showed that the null hypothesis that the relative frequencies of the three functional ceramic classes in the Purcell–Larson and Pinedale areas are samples from the same population could not be rejected. Thus, these tests do not suggest that all Purcell–Larson sites were seasonally occupied sites while the Pinedale sites were permanent habitation sites. This evidence is consistent with the discussion of site sizes in the two areas. Both analyses suggest that the hypothesis that all Chevelon sites were seasonally occupied must be rejected.

Implications of the results for design variation

These results indicate the ceramics present on all Chevelon sites were not deposited during seasonal use of the area by populations in surrounding areas. Thus, design variation in the Chevelon area was not effected in this manner. At the same time, there are aspects of the settlement-subsistence system in the Purcell–Larson area that probably did have an impact on design variability. First, while the analysis has indicated *all* of the sites in the Purcell–Larson area were not seasonally occupied, it is also likely that all the sites were not habitation sites. The figures presented in Table 6.9 show a considerable amount of variation in the relative frequencies of the functional classes at different sites. Different relative frequencies of activities at such sites are thus suggested. Sites such as CS 439 and CS 466 with low frequencies of decorated jars, which have been interpreted as storage vessels, may represent limited activity sites occupied during one part of the year. In contrast, sites such as CS 412 and CS 483 have higher relative frequencies of storage vessels as would be expected on more permanently occupied sites.

Second, artifact densities on the surfaces of sites are low relative to some other areas, such as Black Mesa. Moreover, excavation has shown that Chevelon sites generally lack middens. When middens are present they are shallow. Thus, a significant percentage of the artifacts on many Purcell–Larson sites lie on the surface. If it is assumed that the number of artifacts with a given use life on a site is primarily a function of the number of people that inhabited the site and the length of time the site was occupied (Schiffer 1976:59), then the evidence suggests that even sites that were occupied the year round were inhabited for only a short period of time, perhaps five to ten years.

Table 6.9. *Values of Mann–Whitney U and level of significance for tests of differences between bowls and jars*

Attribute	Mann–Whitney U	Level of significance
Primary forms, percentage of terraces	18.0	0.056
Secondary forms, percentage of sherds with appended forms	19.5	0.123
Secondary forms, percentage of sherds with unappended forms	23.5	0.484
Composition, percentage of sherds with hatched and solid designs	24.0	0.548
Type of hatching, percentage of cross-hatching	26.5	0.945
Line interaction, percentage of parallel lines	26.0	0.842
Line shape, percentage of straight lines	24.0	0.548
Linearity of simple lines, percentage curvilinear	20.0	0.150
Rim decoration, percentage decorated	24.0	0.548
Primary lines, width	16.0	0.016
Hatching line, width	25.0	0.690
Hatch framing line, width	26.0	0.842
Spacing of hatched lines	27.0	1.000

These characteristics of the settlement-subsistence system would have two primary implications in terms of ceramic design variation. First, as argued in Chapter 2, the shorter the period of time that a site is occupied, the greater the number of sites that will be inhabited by a single group of people and the greater will be the spatial distribution of artifacts produced by the group both in total area and in number of sites. As a result, intersite design similarity may be higher in such areas than in areas where sites are inhabited for longer periods of time.

Second, the discussion and the figures presented for Table 6.8 demonstrate a high degree of variability in the relative percentages of vessel forms at different sites. This is particularly the case when body sherds rather than rim sherds are considered. For example, on the five sites included in the intensive design analysis, the percentage of body sherds from bowls varies between 12 and 39 percent. As was argued in Chapter 2, if there are differences in design attributes between vessel forms, then the similarity in designs between different sites will be affected by the frequencies of different vessel forms on the site.

The hypothesis of design differences between different vessel forms was tested using the design information from the five sites for which body sherds were analyzed. A Mann–Whitney test was used to test the null hypothesis of no difference in relative frequencies of design attribute states between bowls and jars. The data used in the tests were the design attribute frequencies for PGM body sherds. The values of the test statistic and their significance levels for the 13 attributes are shown in Table 6.9. The tests showed statistically significant differences in the frequencies of primary terraces relative to primary triangles on bowls and jars and in the average line width on bowls and jars. On each of the five sites, terraces were more frequent relative to triangles on bowls than on jars. With only one exception, the relative percentage of terraces on bowls at all five sites was higher than the frequency on jars at all the sites. Also, the average line width on jars at all five sites was higher than the average line width on bowls from all five sites. Although there were no significant differences between bowls and jars in design composition, Redman (1978:181) has reported greater percentages of solid designs on jars and hatched designs on bowls for some time periods in the Cibola area.

In addition to these statistically significant differences, there are some other consistent relationships that are not statistically significant because of the small sample size. On four of the five sites, appended secondary forms are more frequent on bowls than on jars, the average amount of spacing between hatching lines is lower on bowls, and the frequency of unappended secondary forms is higher on bowls.

In addition to the comparison between jars and bowls, the relative frequencies of the attribute states of primary forms, design composition, and appended secondary forms on jar bodies and jar rims were compared. A Mann–Whitney test was used to test the null hypothesis that the relative frequencies of the attribute states were the same. This null hypothesis was rejected only for the test involving the relative frequency of solid and hatched designs ($U = 15$, significance level = 0.01). Solid and hatched designs are completely absent from the 61 decorated jar rims from the five sites. Carlson (1970:104) has noted a similar difference on St. Johns Black-on-red jars in the Mogollon area.

These tests indicate that design similarities between sites will be affected by functional similarities and differences between the sites. Holding other factors constant, a site with primarily bowls and a site with primarily jars will be less similar in line width and in the relative frequencies of primary forms than two sites on which bowls are the primary form. These results and the previous discussion indicate that settlement-subsistence systems can affect spatial variability in ceramic designs in a number of ways.

7

Temporal variation

The need to study design change over short periods of time has been discussed earlier. I have argued that we presently have little information on this topic, either in the American Southwest or in other areas of the world. It was hoped that tree-ring dates obtained through limited excavation by CARP in 1973 and 1974 would enable me to date precisely several sites with large black-on-white ceramic collections in order to carry out a study of temporal change in design. However, none of the dates obtained was a cutting date (beams with evidence that the last growth ring is present and that thus can be used to date the death of the tree), so it is not possible to pinpoint the construction dates of the sites. In addition, the maximum number of noncutting dates from a single site was three and for most sites only a single date was obtained. It was, therefore, not possible to infer construction dates from the clustering of noncutting dates. [The clustering of noncutting dates has been the only accepted method for inferring construction dates when cutting dates are not available (Bannister 1962, Dean 1978:250).] It is generally argued that little can be said about the construction date of a site from which only one or two noncutting dates were obtained.

This problem was anticipated prior to the 1974 season and an attempt was made to develop an alternative method for estimating construction dates that was not dependent on the number of noncutting dates available. The basic problem with noncutting dates is that an unknown number of outside tree rings are missing. That is, there is a temporal gap between the dated event (the age of the last ring still remaining on the beam) and the important reference event (the date of the death of the tree), to use the terminology recently suggested by Dean (1978:226–8). On the basis of current knowledge, we cannot estimate whether or not there are five rings or thirty rings missing from a beam (Bannister 1962:511–12). Thus, estimates of construction dates for a site, the target event in Dean's terms, cannot be made. It was felt, however, that it might be possible to demonstrate that beams with and without the original outside ring present were chosen by prehistoric people from the same population of trees, that is, trees of the same number of growth rings. If this could be demonstrated, it would suggest that beams with the original outside ring missing have, on the average, as many rings missing as the difference between the mean number of rings on samples with cutting dates and the mean number of rings on samples without cutting dates.

If beams with cutting and noncutting dates were obtained from the same population, two things would be expected. First, the mean number of rings present on noncutting date samples should be *less* than the mean number of rings present on cutting date samples. Second, it would be expected that the variation in the number of rings present on samples without cutting dates would be slightly less or equal to the variation in the number of rings present on samples with cutting dates. If these expectations are not met, then this would suggest that beams with noncutting dates were significantly older (that is, had more rings) than beams with cutting dates. Such a pattern might occur if because of natural or cultural factors, the more rings a beam had, the greater the probability that the outside rings deteriorated or were removed. If the expectations are met, however, it would suggest that, on the average, noncutting date samples originally had as many rings as samples with the outside rings present and thus have only a few rings missing. However, to argue that this is the case for any individual sample would be tenuous, at best, because we are talking about average samples, not individual samples. A more reliable, less risky method would be to make probability statements regarding the noncutting dates on the basis of the sample of beams with cutting dates. For example, we could calculate the maximum number of rings (hereafter referred to as M) present on 95 percent of the beams with cutting dates (assuming for the moment that the pith is present). If noncutting samples and cutting samples were obtained from the same population, it would then be expected that a large percentage of the samples with noncutting dates had no more than M rings originally. (The probability is not exactly 95 percent, inasmuch as we only have a sample from the population of beams with cutting dates. The value of M is thus subject to sampling error; for simplicity, however, the percentage of the samples will be referred to as a "95 percent confidence interval.") For example, if M equals 125 rings, a sample with a noncutting date of 1275 and 100 rings present would have an estimated "95 percent confidence interval" for the construction date of 1275 to 1300.

In order to determine whether or not it is possible to interpret the tree-ring dates from the Chevelon sites in this way, it is first necessary to determine whether or not beams with cutting dates and

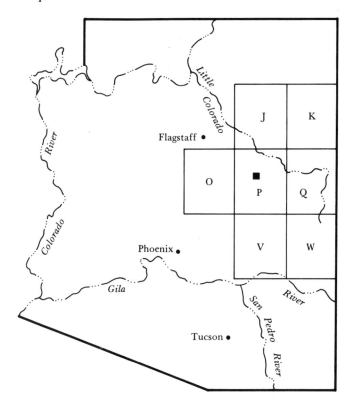

Figure 7.1. Tree-ring areas or quadrangles used by the Laboratory of Tree-Ring Research at the University of Arizona.

beams without cutting dates were selected from the same population. As noted, if this hypothesis is correct, then it would be expected that the mean number of rings on beams with noncutting dates would be less than the mean number of rings on beams with cutting dates. It would also be expected that the variation in the number of rings on samples without the outside ring present would be equal to or slightly less than the variation in the number of rings present on samples with the outside ring present. To determine whether or not these expectations are met, tree-ring dates for area P (Bannister, Gell, and Hannah 1966), the quadrangle in the Laboratory of Tree-Ring Research system in which the Chevelon sites lie, were examined. The location in Arizona of Area P is shown in Figure 7.1. Four types of dates were defined. Type 1 dates were cutting dates (designated after the outside date by the symbols B, G, L, c, and r in the Laboratory of Tree-Ring Research system) with the pith present (designated after the inside date by the symbols p or ±p). Type 2

Table 7.1. *Analysis of number of rings present on four types of tree-ring dates from five area of Arizona*

	Type 1	Type 2	Type 3	Type 4
Area P				
Mean	48.4	46.0	48.6	43.3
Variance	826.6	580.3	442.7	395.3
Sample size	42	80	44	441
Area J				
Mean	52.0	90.8	. . .	. . .
Variance	449.6	2451.0	. . .	. . .
Sample size	129	252	. . .	. . .
Area K				
Mean	58.1	85.2	. . .	. . .
Variance	819.8	1703.5	. . .	. . .
Sample size	332	139	. . .	. . .
Area V				
Mean	62.3	49.4	62.8	52.9
Variance	779.3	783.8	774.6	684.8
Sample size	42	35	37	88
Area W				
Mean	41.3	39.8	43.6	42.9
Variance	164.3	147.8	383.4	241.3
Sample size	135	44	92	95

dates were noncutting dates (designated after the outside date by the symbol vv) with the pith present. Samples with cutting dates with no pith present (designated by the symbols fp, ±, or lack of a symbol following the inside date) were type 3 dates. Finally, samples without cutting dates on which the pith was absent were type 4 dates. Beams for which the Laboratory of Tree-Ring Research made a subjective judgment that the outside date is close to being a cutting date (designated by the symbol v after the outside date) were not included in the analysis.

After defining the types of dates, the number of rings present on all samples of each type from area P was calculated, and the mean number of rings for each type and the variation in the number of rings on beams of each type were computed. These figures are shown in Table 7.1. Two meaningful comparisons can be made to determine whether or not the expectations delineated above are met. First, beams with cutting and noncutting dates on which the pith is present, types 1 and 2, can be compared, inasmuch as the first or center growth ring is present on both types of beams. The figures in Table 7.1 show that the average number of rings on beams of type 2 was slightly less than the average number of rings on beams of type 1, as would be expected if the hypothesis was true. In addition, the variation, as measured by the variance, in the number of rings present on beams of type 2 was less than the variability in the number of rings present on beams of type 1, also as expected. If the hypothesis that the variation within both types of dates is equal is tested using an F-test, the hypothesis cannot be rejected at the 0.05 level of significance. A second comparison can be made between dates of types 3 and 4, cutting and noncutting dates on which the pith is not present. Again, the figures in Table 7.1 indicate that the expectations are met, because the mean and variance of type 4 dates are less than the mean and variance of type 3 dates. If the hypothesis that the variation within both types of dates is equal is tested using an F-test, the hypothesis cannot be rejected at the 0.05 level of significance. Thus, the beams from area P support the hypothesis that beams with cutting and noncutting dates were selected from the same population and, therefore, support the proposed method of inferring construction dates from noncutting dates in area P.

Dates from four surrounding areas, quadrangles J, K, V, and W (Bannister, Robinson, and Warren 1967; Bannister, Hannah, and Robinson 1966; Bannister and Robinson 1971) in the Laboratory of Tree-Ring Research system were also analyzed in order to verify that the results from area P were not anomalous. The locations of these are shown in Figure 7.1. Areas O, Q, and U, which also are near area P, were not included because of the small number of dates available from those areas. Area I was not included because published dates from that area were not available at the time of analysis. In area V and W, all four types of dates were included, and in areas J and K, only types 1 and 2 were considered. The figures for these areas also are shown in Table 7.1. The figures indicate that the hypothesis is valid for areas V and W, but not for areas J and K, where beams with noncutting dates have a larger number of rings on the average than beams with the outside ring present. These results suggest that the hypothesis may be valid for only particular areas of the Southwest. Areas P, V, and W all lie south of the Little Colorado River along the northern and southern slopes of the Mogollon Rim and areas J and K are located in the plateau country north of the Little Colorado River. Different species of trees or different relative frequencies of the same set of species could be an important factor influencing the variation in results between areas, but it was not possible to control for this factor because information on the species of the dated beams is not published.

Now that it has been demonstrated that area P is not anomalous, the estimated construction dates for the Purcell–Larson sites included in the design analysis can be calculated using the method outlined. For beams of type 1, cutting dates with the pith present, 95 percent of the beams have less than 119 rings. This is higher than

Table 7.2. *Tree-ring dates and estimated construction dates for sites in the Purcell–Larson area included in the design analysis*

Site number	Tree-ring dates (A.D.)	Number of rings	Estimated range of site construction (A.D.)	Midpoint (A.D.)
CS 43	1160p–1219vv	59	1240–1282	1261
	1163p–1240vv	77		
CS 412	1104fp–1195vv	91	1195–1223	1209
CS 503	1238p–1281+vv	43	1281–1357	1318
CS 690	1110p–1198vv	88	1198–1229	1213
CS 734	1112p–1191vv	79	1224–1234	1229
	1115p–1201vv	86		
	1111p–1224vv	113		

p = Pith ring present
vv = Noncutting dates
fp = Pith ring not present
+ = One or more rings may be missing near the end of the ring series

either area V or W, where 95 percent of type 1 beams have less than 106 and 64 rings, respectively. Thus, in area P the latest probable construction dates of sites can be estimated by subtracting the number of rings present on a beam from 119 and adding the remainder to the outside date for the beam. The tree-ring dates for the Purcell–Larson sites and the estimated construction dates based on the method described are shown in Table 7.2. As noted previously, these construction dates are consistent with the dating suggested by the independently established seriation of ceramic types. Thus, it is assumed that there are no dating errors resulting from the factors described by Bannister (1962) and Dean (1970) and that the dates of the deaths of the trees are valid estimates of the dates of the construction of the site.

The construction dates suggest the following temporal ordering of sites, proceeding from the oldest to the most recent: CS 412 and CS 690, CS 734, CS 43, and CS 503. Given the large overlap between the estimated periods of construction of CS 412 and CS 690, their temporal position relative to each other cannot be estimated. The temporal order suggested by this analysis is thus the same as that indicated by the latest date for each site before the consideration of the confidence intervals. However, use of the confidence intervals has shown there is a good probability that the ordering reflects the sequence in which the sites were constructed and probably is not affected by the differential preservation of beams and growth rings at any one site relative to the others.

Ceramic information

In addition to the tree-ring dates, other information relevant to the temporal position of the sites must be considered. As Dean (1978: 250) has argued, "the behavioral significance of a single date is uncertain and, in the absence of comparative chronological data provided by other dates, is very difficult to evaluate." As noted in Chapter 3, the ceramic frequency seriation suggested that between A.D. 1150 and 1300, SShO decreased in relative frequency while PGM increased. The relative frequencies of these two classes presented in Table 3.3 show that CS 690 has the highest relative frequency of SShO, followed by CS 503, CS 412, CS 734, and CS 43, in that order. The frequencies for CS 690, CS 412, CS 734, and CS 43 are consistent with the tree-ring dates. In conjunction with the dates, they suggest that CS 690 is the earliest site, followed by CS 412, CS 734, and CS 43.

The relative ceramic frequencies and tree-ring date for CS 503 are not consistent. Although CS 503 has the latest outside tree-ring date and the latest estimated date of site construction, it has the second highest frequency of SShO. This discrepancy may be caused by multiple occupations at the site. While there is only one room block on the sites and no evidence of other structures, the distributions of PGM and SShO on the surface of the sites are different. If we use the information from the random surface collection we see that SShO is concentrated in the southeastern quarter of the site where 49.1 percent of the SShO sherds collected in the sample were found. In this same area were only 24.7 percent of the PGM sherds collected in the sample. The distribution of the two classes on the surface indicates the possibility of two temporally separate occupations of the site. If such was the case, it would account for the discrepancy between the tree-ring date and the relative frequencies of ceramics.

The tests

As a consequence of the discrepancy between the ceramic frequencies and the tree-ring date for CS 503 and the possibility of multiple occupations, CS 503 was eliminated from the analysis of design changes through time. The remaining four sites were then combined into two groups on the basis of the relative ceramic frequencies and the tree-ring dates. These data support the hypothesis that CS 690 and CS 412 were built prior to CS 43 and CS 734. The former sites were thus considered one group and the latter sites were considered a second group.

The attributes and attribute states employed in the tests in Chapters 5 and 6 were used to examine attribute frequencies for each vessel form for PGM sherds, to determine whether or not there

Table 7.3. *Attributes for which there is and is not temporal patterning in the relative frequencies of attribute states*

Attribute	Bowls	Jars
Primary forms, percentage of terraces	Patterned $Z = 1.74^b$	Not patterned
Secondary forms, percentage of sherds with appended forms	Not patterned	Patterned $Z = 1.42$
Secondary forms, percentage of sherds with unappended forms	Patterned $Z = 2.05^a$	Not patterned
Composition, percentage of sherds with hatched and solid designs	Patterned $Z = 2.65^a$	Not patterned
Type of hatching, percentage of cross hatching	Not patterned	Not patterned
Line interaction, percentage of parallel lines	Not patterned	Not patterned
Line shape, percentage of straight lines	Not patterned	Not patterned
Linearity of simple lines, percentage curvilinear	Not patterned	Patterned $Z = 0.80$
Rim decoration, percentage decorated	Not patterned	Not patterned
Primary lines, width	Not patterned	Not patterned
Hatching line, width	Patterned $D = 0.423^a$	Patterned $D = 0.241^a$
Hatched framing line, width	Patterned $D = 0.498^a$	Patterned $D = 0.223^a$
Spacing of hatch lines	Patterned $D = 0.410^a$	Patterned $D = 0.241^a$

[a]Significant at 0.05 level.
[b]Significant at 0.10 level.

is a temporal pattern in the attribute state frequencies. That is, for each attribute and each type of vessel form, type of hatching and jar sherds, for example, I checked to see if the attribute frequencies for CS 734 and CS 43 were *both* lower or were *both* higher than the attribute frequencies for CS 690 and CS 412. In 11 of the 26 cases, there is temporal patterning in the attribute frequencies, as shown in Table 7.3. However, 9 cases would be expected as a result of chance. Thus, considering this evidence alone, the possible cases of temporal patterning cannot be considered statistically significant.

For those cases in which temporal patterning was suggested, the attribute frequencies for CS 43 and CS 734 and for CS 690 and CS 412 were combined. For the width of hatching lines and framing lines and the spacing between hatching lines, attributes measured on a continuous scale, a Kolmogorov–Smirnov test was used to determine whether the differences between the site groups are statistically significant. For the remaining attributes that were measured on a presence-absence scale, a difference in proportions test was used. Of the eleven cases of temporal patterning, these tests indicated that eight are statistically significant at the 0.05 level. Six of the significant changes were on bowl forms. The frequency of primary terraces relative to triangles and the relative frequency of sherds with solid and hatched forms increased through time on bowls, while the frequency of appended secondary forms, the width of hatching lines, the width of framing lines on hatched forms, and the amount of space between hatching lines decreased. The latter three changes also occurred on jars.

Some of these temporal trends are consistent with trends in other parts of the Mogollon area. One of the distinctions between the Wingate design style that is found on Reserve Black-on-white, which dates to the period between A.D. 1000 to 1200, and the subsequent Tularosa design style found on Tularosa Black-on-white (A.D. 1100 to 1300) is a more similar size of solid and hatched forms and narrower spaces between the hatched and solid forms with the Tularosa style (Carlson 1970:90). Carlson (1970: 90) notes that "this permits a greater number of them to be repeated on the field." The more similar sizes of solid and hatched forms and the closer spacing of the forms would increase the probability that both hatched and solid forms would appear on a sherd of a given size. In addition, the Puerco style of design, which also is found on Reserve Black-on-white and dates to the period from A.D. 1000 to 1200, is not characterized by opposed solid and hatched forms (Carlson 1970:89; Wasley 1959:271). Again, this design pattern would decrease the probability on earlier sherds of finding both solid and hatched forms on a single sherd. The trends suggested by these ceramic type descriptions are supported by data from some parts of the Mogollon area. Design attribute analysis by Hantman and Lightfoot (1977) of black-on-white sherds from a 725 square kilometer (280 square mile) area south of Springerville in east-central Arizona and of the ceramic collections made by Danson (1957) in his survey of east-central Arizona and west-central New Mexico showed that hatched forms increased in frequency between A.D. 1000 to 1200. Also, the ceramic type frequencies from the Carter Ranch Site (Longacre 1964b) and Broken K Pueblo (Hill 1970) show that the percentage of sherds with hatched and solid forms increased from about 13 percent to approximately 48 percent between the occupation of the Carter Ranch Site from A.D. 1100 to 1175 and the occupation of Broken K Pueblo from A.D. 1200 to 1300. This study, thus, supports a temporal trend between A.D. 1100 and 1300 in the Mogollon area of an increasing frequency of sherds with both solid and hatched designs.

One of the other temporal trends indicated by these results that also has been suggested previously is the decrease in the amount of space between hatching lines. At the Cibola White Ware Conference (1958), more closely spaced hatching lines was one of the characteristics noted as distinguishing Tularosa Black-on-white from Reserve Black-on-white. For the other attributes for which temporal trends were demonstrated in these tests, supporting evidence is absent in the literature on Mogollon ceramics.

Substantive significance of the tests

While these tests unfortunately have not provided information on rates of design change through time, they have demonstrated statistically significant changes in some design attributes over relatively short periods of time in the Southwest. The average difference between the midpoints of the estimated construction dates for the two groups of sites is 34 years. The maximum difference between the estimated construction dates is 66 years if we take the earliest estimated construction date for CS 412 and CS 690 and the latest estimated construction date for CS 43 and CS 734. Thus, the temporal design changes demonstrated here probably occurred between a period of 34 and 66 years.

This evidence is consistent with an increasing amount of data suggesting relatively rapid design change over short periods of time in the Southwest. Changes in line widths and in other ceramic attributes other than designs have been demonstrated for periods of less than 25 years in the Cibola area of western New Mexico (LeBlanc 1975). In addition, Redman's continuing analysis of design attribute frequencies from the Cibola area has indicated that temporal differences between sites is a primary determinant of intersite similarity in design attribute frequencies (1978:183–4).

Finally, the best evidence for the importance of design change over short periods of time comes from the Black Mesa area of northeastern Arizona. In a study carried out since the completion of the analysis of the Chevelon data, Hantman and I (1978, n.d.) analyzed design attribute frequencies from 24 sites with tree-ring dates. The dates for the sites range from A.D. 815 to 1122. Of the 24 sites, 8 have cutting dates. An attribute-based design classification system similar to the one used for the Chevelon ceramics was employed. Correlating the relative attribute state frequencies with the tree-ring dates revealed strong patterns of covariation for a large percentage of the attribute states. Fourteen of the 53 individual attribute states (26.4 percent) are correlated with the tree-ring dates at higher than the 0.70 or −0.70 levels. Thus, 50 percent or more of their variation is associated with change through time. Twenty-eight of the attribute states (52.8 percent) have correlation coefficients higher than 0.50 or −0.50. If the 16 general attributes are examined, 9 (56.3 percent) have at least one attribute state that is correlated with the tree-ring dates at higher than the 0.70 or −0.70 levels and 13 (81.3 percent) have at least one attribute state higher than 0.60 or −0.60. Only three attributes do not have at least one attribute state that is strongly correlated with the dates. The attributes that are correlated most strongly with the dates are line width, the composition of forms, the linearity of hatching lines, the linearity of hatched forms, and the type of secondary forms. They are very similar to the attributes that were found to be patterned temporally in the Chevelon area.

The Black Mesa data are also more informative than the Chevelon tests in regard to rates of design change. They indicate that change was continuous but did not occur at a constant rate through time. Rather than a linear rate of change, the change over time followed a somewhat curvilinear pattern – as illustrated by two of the scatter plots shown in Figure 7.2. In addition, the scatter plots suggest that design variation over time was not characterized by periods of change followed by periods of stability. As noted earlier, the latter pattern of change has been assumed in those studies (e.g. Longacre 1964a, Tuggle 1970) that have assigned sites to temporal phases on the basis of ceramic type and design frequencies and then have used the degree of design similarity between sites of the same phase to measure interaction intensities. The results of the Chevelon study in combination with the results of LeBlanc, Redman, and Hantman and Plog (1978, n.d.) suggest that design composition and the size of forms, particularly primary lines and hatching lines, are the design attributes that vary in the most consistent manner through time.

These results demonstrate that temporal variation cannot be ignored in design studies, as it has been in many recent analyses that have used design variation to make inferences concerning prehistoric social organization. Data from the Cibola, Black Mesa, and Chevelon areas suggest that change in many design attribute states may have been continuous through time and during at least some periods may have been rapid. Thus, studies in the American Southwest of groups of sites dating to the same temporal phase, even those only 25 to 75 years in duration or studies of individual sites occupied for even brief periods of time, must either consider the temporal dimension or they must focus on those attribute states that do not covary significantly with time. The studies discussed here also support the traditional use of ceramic design variation to date sites in the American Southwest. They suggest that quantitative studies of changes in design attribute frequencies through time ultimately may allow us to date precisely sites on the basis of ceramic collections alone, as Rowe (1959) and LeBlanc (1975) have suggested.

The importance of temporal variation in designs in other areas of the world will need to be established by additional research. As I

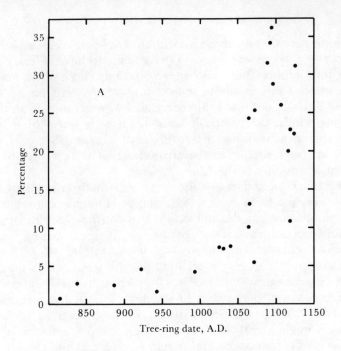

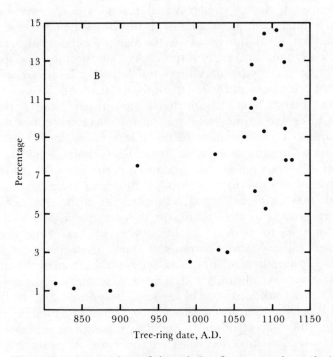

Figure 7.2. Scatterplots of the relative frequency through time of hatched designs (A) and lines between 4.2 and 4.99 mm. in width (B) on ceramics from tree-ring dated sites from Black Mesa, Arizona.

have suggested elsewhere (S. Plog 1976b:270, 272), there appear to
be differences between areas in rates of design change over time.
For example, prehistoric ceramic designs from the Valley of Oaxaca
in Mexico, which may have had religious significance, appear to
have very low rates of change over time and stronger patterns of
regional and intrasite spatial patterns (S. Plog 1976b, Pyne 1976) in
comparison to prehistoric ceramic designs from the American
Southwest that are not known to have had religious significance.
This difference in change rate suggests that the social context of the
manufacture and use of ceramic designs is an important factor that
must be considered in studies of design variation, as Binford
(1965:206) has suggested. Unfortunately, it is a factor that has received little attention in comparisons of patterns of design variation
in different areas of the world.

8

Theories of style and ceramic design variation

The tests presented in Chapters 6, 7, and 8 support the hypotheses presented in Chapter 2. The tests show that ceramic exchange, temporal variation, and stylistic differences between different vessel forms all account for part of the ceramic design variation at the sites included in the analysis. In addition, arguments for the importance of considering settlement-subsistence systems in explanations of stylistic variation are presented.

The results of the tests are summarized in Table 8.1; the table indicates that of temporal variation, vessel form, and exchange, the latter variable accounts for the most significant differences in the design attribute state frequencies on ceramics from Chevelon sites. There are significant differences between two pottery classes, PGM and SShO, in the relative frequencies of different primary forms, types of design composition, and type of hatching; in the frequency of appended secondary forms and rim decoration; and in the size of primary lines, hatching lines, framing lines, and the spacing of hatching lines. The co-occurrence of these two classes on Chevelon sites is a result of the importation of SShO vessels, most likely from the area around Winslow. The two pottery classes are characteristic of two cultural traditions in the American Southwest, the Winslow branch of the Anasazi and the Mogollon.

The second most important factor in accounting for statistically significant differences in Chevelon design attribute frequencies was temporal variation. Variation through time was demonstrated in the relative frequencies on at least one of the two vessel forms of different primary forms and types of composition, in the frequency of unappended secondary forms, and in the size of hatching lines, framing lines, and spacing of hatching lines.

Design differences between different vessel forms accounted for the smallest number of statistically significant differences in attribute state frequencies. Relative frequencies of primary forms and the size of line widths were significantly different on bowls versus jars, and

Table 8.1. *Attributes with statistically significant differences between pottery classes or vessel forms or temporal groups of sites*

Attribute	Vessel form	Bowl Time	Bowl Pottery class (PGM SSho)	Jar Time	Jar Pottery class (PGM SSho)
Primary forms, percentage of terraces	*	*	*	NS	NS
Secondary forms, percentage of sherds with appended forms	*	NS	NS	NS	*
Secondary forms, percentage of sherds with unappended forms	NS	*	NS	NS	NS
Composition, percentage of sherds with solid and hatched designs	*	*	NS	NS	*
Type of hatching, percentage of cross-hatching	NS	NS	*	NS	NS
Line interaction, percentage of parallel lines	NS	NS	NS	NS	NS
Line shape, percentage of straight lines	NS	NS	NS	NS	NS
Linearity of simple line, percentage curvilinear	NS	NS	NS	NS	NS
Rim decoration, percentage decorated	NS	NS	*	NS	*
Primary line, width	*	NS	NS	NS	*
Hatching line, width	NS	*	*	*	*
Hatched framing line, width	NS	*	*	*	*
Spacing of hatching lines	NS	*	*	*	*

* = Statistically significant difference or trend, significant at 0.10.
NS = Not significant.

differences in design composition were found between jar bodies and jar necks.

Of 13 design attributes considered, part of the variation in 10 was accounted for by at least one of the three factors. Only variation in types of line interaction, line shape, and rectilinear versus curvilinear designs were not accounted for by any of the factors. The 10 attributes for which part of the variability was accounted for have been some of the major aspects of design variation that have been analyzed in previous design studies. For example, inspection of the previous design elements used in the design-based studies of social organization by Hill (1970), Longacre (1970) and others indicates that alternative states of the 10 attributes were the primary distinctions defining the design elements used in these studies. It is very probable, therefore, that a significant part of the variation in design element frequencies at the Carter Ranch Site and Broken K Pueblo could be explained by the three factors emphasized in this study. Future studies to determine socially related aspects of design variation should either control for these factors or demonstrate that they are not significant causes of the variation. In addition, alternative states of the 10 attributes are also distinctions that are a major part of the definitions of different pottery types in the American Southwest, types which are assumed to have temporal significance. This study has demonstrated that while some of these attributes do vary in frequency through time, their frequency is also affected in some cases by other factors, such as vessel form, that may need to be controlled if these attribute frequencies are to be used to date sites. For example, while the relative frequency of terraces varies significantly through time on PGM bowls in Chevelon, it also varies between bowls and jars. If the relative frequency of terraces through time had been studied using both vessel forms combined, this temporal trend would have been obscured. Alternatively, differences between sites that would seriate perfectly and would thus appear to be temporally determined could be created by different relative frequencies of vessel forms on the sites because of differing site functions.

Kintigh (1979:48) has argued that it would be unworkable to attempt to control all of these factors in the manner I have suggested. He takes this position because he feels that sample sizes would be too small in intrasite design analyses; for example, if we could only analyze variation on pottery of particular form and a particular class or type (1979:48). I do not think Kintigh's argument is reasonable. To ignore alternative explanatory hypotheses that have been shown by previous research to be important and to pretend that they do not account for significant percentages of the variation observed is scientifically unwise and can only result in spurious conclusions, as I have shown in the brief examples just presented. In addition, in instances in which some of the alternative hypotheses are not important, sample sizes may not be reduced significantly. In fact, the tests presented earlier indicated that all three of the hypotheses tested do not each account for variation in some of the stylistic attributes.

The results of this study have increased our understanding of why ceramic designs vary between sites, but it is also important that we develop and test explanations of stylistic variation in general. As noted, the research conducted in this study was not directed toward this question, dealing instead with the specific question of why there is spatial variation in ceramic designs. In the remainder of this chapter, the perspective will be expanded. The question of why ceramic designs vary, that is, why different vessels of the same form and date painted by different potters have similar or different designs will be considered.

The primary theories concerning stylistic variation will be reviewed first. Next, information on the evolution of design variation in the American Southwest as a whole will be presented in order to evaluate the theories discussed. It will also be necessary to present an overview of particular aspects of cultural evolution in the Southwest. Finally, I will attempt to integrate the conclusions drawn from this summary with studies in other areas and with some of the conclusions of the research presented here.

Theories of stylistic variation
At least five major explanations of stylistic variation have been developed. In the following discussion, these will be called *normative theory* (Binford 1965), *stylistic drift* (Binford 1963; Cleland 1972), *social interaction* (Deetz 1965; Hill 1970; Longacre 1970; and Whallon 1968 among others), *motor habit variation* (Hill 1977, 1978), and *information exchange* (Wobst 1977). While I consider these separate theories, the first three are very similar in many ways. All three emphasize the importance of learning in the transmission of varieties of stylistic behavior. For example, in his description of normative theory, Binford (1965:204) argues that normative theorists believe that "learning is the recognized basis of transmission between generations and diffusion is the basis of transmission between social units not linked by regular breeding behavior." The social interaction theory, as formulated in the research of Deetz (1965), Longacre (1970), and others (Hill 1970; Whallon 1968) emphasizes similar ideas, as I have argued in previous sections. Binford's (1963:91–2) discussion of the concept of cultural drift also is based on the assumption that "the range and stability of individual variation in the execution of stylistic norms between parent and daughter communities is a function of the generational continuity in learning and enculturation between the populations." In addition to the common stress on learning, these three theories also emphasize the importance of interaction between individuals in the transmission of ideas through space. Binford (1965:204) argues that normative theorists believed that "culture is transmitted between generations and across breeding populations in inverse proportion to the degree of social distance maintained between the groups in question." As a result, spatial discontinuities in the distribution of similar stylistic elements were interpreted frequently by nor-

mative theorists as resulting from "natural barriers to social intercourse" (Binford 1965:204) or from social or cultural boundaries
(Wobst 1977:328). Similarly, Whallon (1968:223) states that

> the nature of the diffusion of stylistic practices, both
> within and between communities, will be determined by
> the nature of interaction among artisans. The aspect of
> style concerned, the rate of diffusion, and the directions
> and limits of diffusion will be conditioned by the kind,
> frequency, and channeling of interaction among the pro-
> ducers of the stylistic material.

Although these three theories of style all emphasize the importance of learning and interaction in the transmission of stylistic elements, they differ in their view of the locus of stylistic behavior.
Because of the view of normative theories that culture is shared and
homogeneous (Hill 1970:17; Binford 1965:203–4), broad culture
areas are thought to be characterized by a single norm or idea concerning stylistic behavior such as the types of designs to be painted
on a pot.

Binford's discussion of culture drift recognizes social units of different sizes as the loci of stylistic variation. He argues that stylistic
variation is a result of the social context of the artisans making the
artifacts, the social context in which the artifacts are used, or both
(1965:206). These distinctions are particularly important, he argues,
"if the social context of manufacture or use are not isomorphic, as in
the case of items circulated widely through exchange systems, or
used primarily in the context of institutions functioning for interso-
cietal articulation." As a result, the locus of stylistic variation may
reside in social units of differing scales. "This variation may arise
from a traditional way of doing things within a family or a larger
social unit, or it may serve as a conscious expression of between-
group solidarity" (1965:206).

More recent analyses of stylistic variation have emphasized social
interaction between individuals as the primary determinant of the
variation, as documented extensively in earlier chapters. The locus
of variation is the individual. Individuals will paint designs like other
individuals to the degree that the individuals interact. As individuals
have varying spheres of interaction with other individuals that are
determined by organizational units such as residence groups, lineages, clans, villages, intervillage alliances, and intravalley alliances,
it can be expected that varying degrees of stylistic similarity can be
found at different spatial scales that reflect these units. For example,
design difference between different rooms within a pueblo may be
indicative of uxorilocal residence groups. This viewpoint has been
summarized as follows:

Social demography and social organization are reflected in the material system. In a society practicing post-marital rules stressing matrilocality, social demography may be mirrored in the ceramic art of female potters; the smaller and more closely tied the social aggregate, the more details of design will be shared. Augmented by clues from other aspects of the cultural system differential relative frequencies of designs may suggest the delimitation of various social aggregates; larger social units such as the villages interacting in a relatively large area and producing pottery of the same Variety or Type; groups of villages forming a unit through social interaction along kin-based, religious, and political lines; the village as a social group; and residence groups forming a village [Longacre 1970:28].

As Aberle (1970:217) has noted, this viewpoint emphasizes the concept of norms in a manner similar to normative theory. The difference between the viewpoints thus is not in the emphasis on norms, but rather in the arguments for broad norms, those of a large social group, versus narrower norms, those of individuals (Aberle 1970:217).

An additional explanation of variation in some stylistic attributes has been proposed by Hill (1977, 1978) and others [cf. many of the articles in Hill and Gunn (1977)]. Hill (1977:100) suggests that differences between individuals in motor habits are the primary source of variation in a number of attributes such as the angle at which designs intersect, "the relative heights or lengths of portions of a design," the widths and distances between lines, and the area and shape of parts of designs. It is proposed (Hill 1977, 1978) that variation in the execution of such design characteristics is subconscious and, in contrast to the other explanations of stylistic variation just discussed, is not affected by the intensity of interaction between individuals or the context of learning the production of a craft. Thus, Hill has suggested that variation in the design attributes listed here can be used to isolate the products of individual perhistoric artisans.

A final theory of style that emphasizes the role of stylistic variation in information exchange has been developed primarily by Wobst (1977). In addition, Braun (1977:117) has suggested that informal discussions of some of the major concepts of the information exchange theory have been presented by Kroeber and Richardson (1940), Kroeber (1963), Friedrich (1970), and Wilmsen (1973). Some of the proposals of Binford (1963, 1965) noted previously are also incorporated into this theory. Braun (1977:118) states that these authors emphasize that "stylistic" behavior, as a *cultural* phenomenon, should be investigated in terms of the "function" such behavior performs as it articulates with other cultural variables in a "systemic matrix" (Wobst 1977:317–319). At the most general level, these works argue that the decoration of domestic products, dress, and surroundings is a form of social display or advertising behavior, encoding information not only about the identity of the maker or user, but also potentially about his social group membership, status, wealth, religious beliefs and political ideology.

For example, Wobst (1977:322) suggests that stylistic messages "contribute heavily to human survival." He suggests, however, that the cost of artifact production and the cost of decoding messages will inhibit stylistic messages from being used to transmit a wide variety of information, in order to lower the relative cost per message (1977:323). Messages of social group affiliation (Binford 1965:206), of ownership, and of religious and political objectification are types of "invariate and recurrent" messages that would be expected to be transmitted stylistically (Wobst 1977:323). Such messages may play an important role in social integration by linking

> those members of a community particularly efficiently who are not in constant verbal contact and who have little opportunity to observe each other's behavior patterns . . . Stylistic messaging defines mutually expectable behavior patterns and makes subsequent interaction more predictable and less stressful . . . Thus, an important function of stylistic messaging derives from the fact that it makes social intercourse more predictable: it reduces the stress inherent in first or intermittent encounters, and it broadcasts the potential advantages or disadvantages to be realized from a more intimate encounter, before such encounter has taken place [Wobst 1977:327].

> If, through the messages on his clothing, home, and other artifacts, an individual says: "I am an individual that belongs to social group X," he is also saying that he is in conformity with the other behavioral norms and with the ideology behind these norms [Wobst 1977:327–8].

Two important aspects of the information exchange theory in regard to predicting stylistic variation on artifacts are the amount of contact with socially distant people and the visibility of the artifacts. First, Wobst (1977:323) argues that the utility of stylistic messages decreases with decreasing social distance between the sender and receiver, inasmuch as there would be fewer messages that could not be transmitted more cheaply using another mode of communication. Stylistic messages thus

> gain in utility relative to other modes, if the potential receivers have little opportunity to receive the message otherwise, but nevertheless are likely to encounter it and are able to encode it. This circumscribes a potential target of receivers intermediate in social distance to the emitter of the message: not too close – since the message usually would be known already or generally could be more easily transmitted in other communication modes, and not too distant – since decoding or encountering the message could not be assured [Wobst 1977:323–4].

Therefore, Wobst (1977:326) argues that the quantity of stylistic behavior will increase as the size of the social network in which an individual participates increases. From this viewpoint, he argues that given the small social networks of band societies, it is not surprising "that the functional matrix for stylistic behavior is only weakly developed" (1977:326).

Second, the information exchange theory emphasizes the importance of the visibility of artifacts, because it is those artifacts seen by more individuals that are most appropriate for the transmission of stylistic messages (Wobst 1977:330).

> those specific stylistic forms will have the widest distribution which are affixed to artifacts which are the most visible and the most accessible to other individuals . . . specific stylistic forms will be clinally distributed within and between social units if they are seen only by a relatively small number of individuals . . . social-group specific stylistic form should occur only among the messages which are most widely broadcast, which broadcast signals of group affiliation, and which enter into processes of boundary maintenance [Wobst 1977:330].

This emphasis on artifact visibility is similar to Binford's (1965:206) arguments noted earlier, concerning the importance of the social context of artifact use and manufacture. It is also similar to the proposals of Deetz and others in its suggestion that stylistic forms on low visibility artifacts will be clinally distributed. The information exchange theory, thus, incorporates aspects of other theories while elaborating upon them and providing a more encompassing rationale for stylistic variation.

Spatial and temporal variation in style: theoretical expectations
Expectations concerning how stylistic forms should vary through space and time can be deduced from some of the theories already

given. The theory developed by Deetz (1965) and others suggests that differences in designs will be found between spatial units on a very small scale such as between rooms within a pueblo. They also suggest that difference will occur between different valleys and between other units on a larger scale. As I have argued in previous sections and elsewhere (1976b), this theory basically predicts that because of the channeling of interaction by organizational units and the effects of distance on interaction intensities, the greater the physical distance between two spatial units such as rooms or sites, the lower will be the degree of stylistic similarity between the units. The information exchange theory also predicts a clinal distribution of stylistic forms when the artifacts are not highly visible or when they will not be encountered by many socially distant individuals. However, if the artifacts are visible and are seen by socially distant people, the information exchange theory predicts that such artifacts may have social group specific stylistic forms. Thus, the social context of ceramic manufacture and use must be considered. In such cases, there may be a homogeneous distribution of stylistic forms over the space occupied by the social group. Similarly, normative theory also predicts such a homogeneous distribution within the area occupied by a given social unit. Finally, if stylistic variation is primarily determined by individual variation in motor habits that are subconscious and cannot be shared, a random pattern of variation through space would be expected.

Expectations concerning variation through time are dependent on changes in other variables. The social interaction theory would predict changes in intrasite and intersite design variability with changes in interaction intensities, changes in organizational units such as residence groups or lineages, or changes in marital rules such as village endogamy. Changes in ceramic visibility, in the context of ceramic manufacture and use, and in the size of social networks that individuals participate in should affect stylistic behavior, according to the information exchange theory. Expectations concerning temporal changes that can be deduced from normative theory have been described by Binford (1965:204):

> Formal changes in the temporal distribution of items are viewed as the result of innovations or the operation of a built-in dynamics sometimes designated as "drift" (Ford, 1954, p. 51; Herskovits, 1958, pp. 581–582) . . . Both innovation and drift are considered natural to culture, and as Caldwell (1958, p. 1) has said, "other things being equal, changes in material culture through time and space will tend to be regular." Discontinuities in rates of change or in formal continuity through time are viewed as the

result of historical events which tends to change the configuration of social units through such mechanisms as ex-
tensions of trade, migration, and the diffusions of "core"
ideas such as religious cult (Ritchie, 1955).

Binford (1963) also has outlined temporal changes in stylistic variation that might occur as a result of cultural drift. If major demographic increases occur with population budding and the establishment of daughter communities, random sampling error would result
in a

> demonstrable pattern of covariation between formal dif-
> ferences characteristic of spatially separated units. Covaria-
> tion relationships between differences in separate attri-
> butes or normative classes should overlap in regular spatial
> patterns, resulting in a radiating or linear distribution
> (Binford 1963:93–4).

In stable demographic situations, stylistic drift would occur primarily

> as a result of random sampling error in the degree to
> which individual variants are disproportionally repre-
> sented between the parent and descendent populations.
> Changes arising in this manner automatically result in a
> slightly modified statistical norm in the daughter commu-
> nity. Such a shift may remain a purely statistical pheno-
> mena or may, under selection for maximizing the material
> means of group identification, be objectified and elabo-
> rated, thereby serving the functions of enhancing group
> solidarity (Binford 1963:92).

Cleland (1972:209) also suggests that objects such as pottery, which
have a short use life and which are mobile, will undergo rapid style
change over time as a result of drift. Finally, motor habit variation
also should result in random change through time as well as through
space.

Now that theoretical expectations concerning spatial and temporal
stylistic variability have been discussed, the empirical data concerning spatial and temporal ceramic design variation in the American
Southwest will be presented. Only the northern part of the Southwest, north of the Mogollon Rim, will be considered because few
studies of design variation have been made elsewhere. Locations of
many of the areas mentioned in the following discussion are shown
in Figure 8.1. After this evidence is discussed, it will be necessary to
discuss demographic changes, social networks, social interaction, and
ceramic visibility and the social context of ceramic manufacture and
use. Finally, these data will be used to evaluate the predictions of
different theories of style.

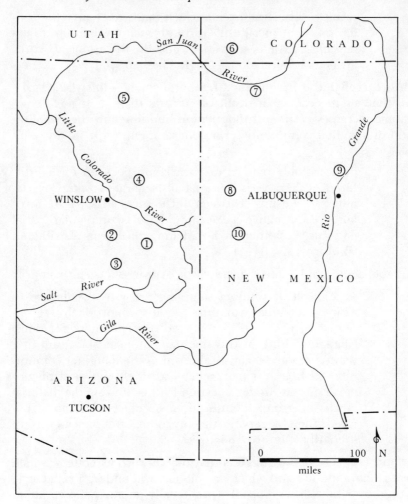

Figure 8.1. Map of the American Southwest showing the location of several of the areas discussed in the text: (1) Hay Hollow Valley, (2) Purcell–Larson region, (3) Grasshopper area, (4) Hopi Buttes region, (5) northern Black Mesa, (6) Mesa Verde, (7) Salmon Ruin area, (8) Cibola–El Morro region, (9) Rio Grande Valley, and (10) the Upper Gila region.

Spatial variation in prehistoric Southwestern ceramic designs

The question to be addressed in this section is the spatial scale at which differences in ceramic designs occur in the Southwest. A small scale, within site differences, will be considered first and then progressively larger spatial units will be discussed.

Only a few studies have attempted to determine whether nonrandom spatial clusters of ceramic designs are present within contemporaneous areas of a single prehistoric site in the Southwest. These are

Hill's (1970) study of Broken K, Longacre's (1970) analysis of the
Carter Ranch Site, the research at Davis Ranch and Reeve Ruin by
Gerald (1975), Clemen's (1976) study of a site on Black Mesa in
northeastern Arizona, Kintigh's (1979) research in the Cibola area of
New Mexico, and Washburn's (1977) tests for differences in design
attribute frequencies within a site in the Upper Gila area of New
Mexico. All but the latter study, in which no intrasite design differences were found (Washburn 1977:173–89), purport to have demonstrated nonrandom spatial clusters of designs within the sites in
question. However, there are several problems with these studies. As
noted, reanalysis of the data from Broken K Pueblo and the Carter
Ranch Site has demonstrated that the reality of the clusters isolated
by Hill and Longacre is very questionable (S. Plog 1976a). The study
of Clemen is based on invalid statistics such as the calculation of
chi-square values from tables in which the expected frequency for
most of the cells is less than five. To use the chi-square statistics,
some statisticians argue that only 20 percent of the cells in a table
should have an expected frequency of less than five (Dixon and
Massey 1969:241). Finally, except for the research of Kintigh (1979),
none of the studies considered in detail alternative explanations of
design variation other than the social interaction theory.

In addition, few if any of the factors discussed in the body of this
study were considered. For example, Kintigh's data included design
attribute frequencies on sherds of St. Johns Black-on-red and St.
Johns Polychrome, two pottery types that have been hypothesized to
have been widely traded in the American Southwest. Also, of the
three rooms at one site that he suggests (1979:48–51, 54) are distinct
stylistically and that he interprets as different residential units or
households, one is very different from the other two in the relative
frequencies of different vessel forms [66 and 69 percent bowls in
two rooms versus 35 percent bowls in the other, according to figures
presented by Redman (1978: Table 8.3)]. Given the results of the
tests presented in Chapter 6, it is possible that one source of the
stylistic differences between these rooms is the different relative
frequencies of vessel forms in the rooms. This seems particularly
likely, given that two of the stylistic characteristics that distinguish
the room with the small percentage of bowls from other rooms are
different relative frequencies of the attribute states of design composition and design form (Kintigh 1979:48). The tests in Chapter 6
have indicated significant differences between bowls and jars in the
relative frequencies of the attribute states for design composition
and design form. For the site analyzed by Kintigh, Redman
(1978:181) found differences between bowls and jars in design composition. The different relative frequencies of vessel forms may in
turn be a result of different activities having been carried out in the

rooms. Consistent with this hypothesis is the fact that the room with the low percentage of bowls is also smaller than the other rooms (Redman 1978:186). Given these problems, I would argue that it has not been demonstrated adequately that nonrandom spatial style clusters existed within contemporaneous parts of prehistoric villages.

If nonrandom clusters do not exist within pueblos, the question of whether or not it can be demonstrated that designs painted on vessels from the same site are more similar than designs painted on vessels from different sites must be considered. The assumption that the latter proposition is true was one of the primary reasons for the proposal by Longacre and others that the degree of social interaction determined stylistic similarities between individuals. The study of Cronin (1962) has been regarded as supporting the proposition (Binford 1965:207; Longacre 1970:27). However, reanalysis of Cronin's data (S. Plog 1976a) has demonstrated that her data do not show that designs on different pottery types from the same site are more similar than designs on the same pottery type from different sites, as has been argued. Tuggle (1970) also has tested this proposition using ceramic data from the Grasshopper area and has demonstrated that it is not valid. Similarly, the evidence presented earlier concerning design difference between Little Colorado and Cibola White Wares from the Chevelon area also does not support the proposition. One study whose conclusions are not consistent with these, however, is Kintigh's. His analysis (1979:45–8) of ceramic designs from several areas within each of three sites in the Cibola area has suggested greater similarity within than between sites for some design attributes. However, as noted, there are several weaknesses in his analysis, particularly the lack of control of other possible explanatory variables. Thus, while I feel Kintigh's study is an important one, for reasons that will be discussed below, the lack of adequate controls reduces the strength of his conclusions. Given the results of all of these studies, it cannot be stated that designs on ceramic vessels from the same site are more similar than designs on vessels from different sites.

Studies of ceramic design variation over larger areas in which sites were located up to about 40 kilometers apart have been made in the Hay Hollow Valley (Longacre 1964a), Chevelon Canyon (S. Plog 1976b), the Grasshopper area (Tuggle 1970), and in northwestern New Mexico and southwestern Colorado (Washburn and Matson 1980). Longacre argued that in the Hay Hollow Valley two spatial clusters of sites existed with different relative frequencies of design elements. Reanalysis of these data, however, has indicated that the clusters suggested by Longacre did not exist (S. Plog 1976a). Analysis of design distributions in the Chevelon Canyon, Hay Hollow Valley, and Grasshopper areas indicated that design similarities between sites also did not correlate with the distance between sites as one would expect if the social interaction theory was correct (S. Plog 1976b). Finally, Washburn and Matsons' (1979) study of design symmetry frequencies on ceramics from groups of sites on Mesa Verde in southwestern Colorado and in northwestern New Mexico suggested to them a correspondence between the geographical and stylistic distances between sites. However, no estimate of statistical significance is possible for one correspondence measure and their other measure considers one spatial axis instead of two. For the sites in northwestern New Mexico, I have calculated the degree of correlation and found it to be low (0.19) and statistically insignificant. At the same time, the correlation for the Mesa Verde sites [with geographical distances measured on a map provided by Hayes (1964: map 3, section 2) and stylistic distances measured on figure 8 in Washburn and Matson (1980)] is both high (0.60) and statistically significant at the 0.05 level. Thus, the vast majority of the studies do not suggest spatial patterning in design distributions at the scale dealt with in the studies covered here. It must be kept in mind, however, that the subjective design classifications that were used in most of these analyses may have obscured any patterning that did exist. Only Washburn and Matson used an objective, attribute analysis and the positive correlation between stylistic and geographical distance for the Mesa Verde sites could be significant in that light.

There has been only one systematic quantitative study of ceramic design variation over areas of the American Southwest larger than those already discussed. Washburn (1978) compared design symmetry frequencies on ceramics from the El Morro, Upper Gila, and Salmon Ruin areas. The latter regions are over 175 kilometers apart while the former areas are about 40 kilometers from each other. Washburn's analysis (1978:112–19) suggested the El Morro and Upper Gila areas were more similar to each other in design symmetry frequencies than were the Salmon Ruin and El Morro or Upper Gila areas. However, Kintigh (1979:59–60) has shown that all of Washburn's data are not consistent with her conclusions.

Other than Washburn's study, we can only rely on general statements about design distributions over large areas. These statements are summaries of subjective impressions rather than objective studies. Yet these impressions are based on a large amount of data. Although spatial patterns in design differences between sites separated up to 40 kilometers have not been demonstrated consistently, evidence does indicate design differences between sites 50 kilometers apart. One example is design distributions in the Chevelon area. Within the Purcell–Larson area, Cibola White Ware ceramics probably were made locally, as suggested earlier. However, in the Winslow

area, only 51 kilometers from Purcell–Larson, Little Colorado White
Wares are found with different designs than those found on Cibola
White Wares. Differences across similar distances can be found also
within a region where a single ware is made. Longacre (1962) has
noted that within an area surveyed during 1960, "design elements
made up of balanced and opposed solids are most abundant" in the
western part of the area near Snowflake, while "design elements
made up of solids and hachured scrolls" were predominate in the
eastern extreme of the area around Springerville at the same time
period. Excavation in the two areas prior and subsequent to Longacre's survey has demonstrated the validity of Longacre's statement
(Rinaldo 1959; Martin, Rinaldo, and Longacre 1961b; Martin et al.
1962, 1964; Martin, Longacre, and Hill 1967). Thus, some studies
indicate that at least in parts of the American Southwest there were
differences in ceramic designs found on pottery from sites separated
by 50 to 85 kilometers.

Design variation across distances greater than this need not be
discussed in detail. That ceramic design differences exist between
areas separated by such distances has been recognized since the
1920s, when several intensive studies of different parts of the Southwest had been completed. These design differences were one aspect
of the information used by Kidder (1972) in 1924 to divide the
Southwest into different cultures, and they have been one of the
traits emphasized by many archaeologists attempting similar divisions in the American Southwest. Thus, information on spatial variation in designs has demonstrated differences in the designs painted
on pottery from areas separated by as little as 50 kilometers. However, it has not been demonstrated consistently that patterned ceramic design differences exist between areas separated by distances
smaller than this.

Temporal variation in prehistoric Southwestern ceramic designs
In addition to examining spatial variation in ceramic designs, it is
also important to examine temporal variation in the evolution of
spatial patterns. Such variation did occur and will be described in
order that the ability of different theories of design to explain it can
be evaluated.

The first types of styles of design painted on black-on-white pottery in the American Southwest were the Lino and Kana-a styles.
Wasley (1959) and Colton (1953) have described the attributes of
these styles. Wasley (1959:229) lists the various pottery types on
which the Lino style is found and notes that the Lino style "characterized all Basketmaker III painted pottery" (1959:245). That is,
different pottery types have been defined for different parts of the
Southwest during the Basketmaker III period (about A.D. 400 to

700), but these types are different from each other in attributes other than the designs painted on them. Similarly, the Kana-a style is found on all Pueblo I (A.D. 700 to 900) pottery types in the American Southwest, although Wasley does suggest two major centers of development for the style (1959:229). During the succeeding Pueblo II period (A.D. 900 to 1100), Wasley argues that the situation changed. While noting that one design style, the Black Mesa style, can be found throughout the Anasazi area (1959:290), he states also that it is only one of many styles that can be delineated during the Pueblo II period, such as the Puerco style, which has a much more localized distribution than previous styles (1959:255, 272).

> It is evident that a single major style dominated the ceramics of each of these two stages of Anasazi development, the Lino style during Basketmaker III and the Kana-a style during Pueblo I.
> This situation is in sharp contrast to that of Pueblo II, which was characterized throughout by three major styles and by two other styles in the last half [Wasley 1959:292].

This trend toward the development of localized design styles has been noted by others also. Roberts (1931:133–4) states that during Pueblo I (A.D. 700 to 900) the black-on-white decorative patterns were widespread, but during late Pueblo II (A.D. 900 to 1100) and Pueblo III (A.D. 1100 to 1300) there was a "pronounced development of characteristic and specialized local form." In their study of ceramic designs from northeastern Arizona, Beals, Brainerd, and Smith (1945:98–9) noted that during Pueblo I (A.D. 700 to 900) there was little regional variation throughout the Pueblo culture area, when compared with the distinctive regional styles that developed later, a conclusion also reached by Guthe (1925:8). They argue that Pueblo II (A.D. 900 to 1100) pottery was more varied than any other period and suggest that this was a result of "more marked cultural intermingling" during the period (Beals, Brainerd, and Smith 1945:99). Similarly, Colton (1939:59) states that "until about 900 A.D., north of the Little Colorado River, the Anasazi in northern Arizona seemed to have had a more or less uniform culture." After this time, Colton suggests that two different branches can be isolated in the area on the basis of ceramics. Finally, Danson (1957:90–2) has described a similar development in east-central Arizona and west-central New Mexico. After A.D. 800 to 900, when a single black-on-white ceramic type characterized the entire area, "the local patterns seem to have developed along their own lines, and areal differences can be detected between the various types of black-on-white wares." He notes, however, that all the types had many similarities in design (1957:92). It was during this time that

populations in the area "spread out into every area where argicul-
ture could be practiced" (1957:104).

Thus, the trend as described by Wasley and others is from a
greater similarity of designs over a broad area to a lesser degree of
similarity through time. During the period from A.D. 900 to 1100,
regional design traditions developed within the American Southwest. Thus, the style zones that were discussed in the section on
spatial variation are primarily characteristic of time periods after
A.D. 900 to 1000.

This statement is consistent with the evidence presented earlier,
where the design differences noted between the Purcell–Larson and
Winslow areas within the Chevelon regions were *not* present at A.D.
900. While pottery painted with mineral paint characteristic of Cibola White Ware and pottery painted with organic paint characteristic
of Tusayan White Ware were both present at that date, the designs
painted with the different types of paint were similar. By A.D. 1100,
the pottery of the two wares was not painted with similar designs.
Thus, the northern part of the American Southwest was characterized by a trend toward greater differences in ceramic designs between different areas through time.

At the same time that regional styles were developing in the
American Southwest, evidence suggests that design similarity between sites *within* a single regional style zone was increasing. The
evidence is sparse but it is consistent. Tuggle's (1970) analysis of sites
in the Grasshopper area of east-central Arizona dating between A.D.
950 to 1400 is the most in-depth analysis. After dividing the sites
into three time periods, the similarity between sites of the same
period was calculated. The results showed that through time there
was increasing similarity between sites of the same temporal period
(Tuggle 1970:84–5). Although this interpretation is not without
problems (see S. Plog 1976a), other data are consistent with it.
Tuggle's limited analysis of design data from late sites in the Pinedale and Snowflake areas of east-central Arizona suggests a similar
pattern (Tuggle 1970:88). Analysis of several sites in the Hay Hollow
Valley dating between A.D. 900 to 1200 also has shown increasing
design similarity through time (Wiley 1971). Finally, Table 8.2 shows
the average similarity between sites in the Hay Hollow Valley and
Mesa Redonda areas calculated from data collected by Longacre
(1964a); these figures also show that design similarity between sites
increased through time.

Thus, available data suggests that between A.D. 900 and 1450
regional ceramic design styles developed in the American Southwest
and that within the developing style zones there was increasing ceramic design similarity between sites. Associated changes in other
important variables will now be considered.

Table 8.2. *Average design similarity between sites with the same estimated period of occupation in the Hay Hollow Valley and Mesa Redonda areas*

Period of occupation	Average Brainerd–Robinson coefficient	Average correlation coefficient
A.D. 700–1100	96.0	0.67
A.D. 900–1100	95.7	0.77
A.D. 900–1300	113.0	0.84

Population and social networks

Ceramic design similarities between areas were varying through time, and changes in many other aspects of cultural systems in the prehistoric American Southwest also were changing. To ultimately suggest an explanation of why design variations were occurring, it is first necessary to discuss these associated changes. In this section, the development in population, mobility, and social networks will be emphasized.

One of the best documented changes that has been discussed in many studies is that of population. In almost every area where archaeological work has been done in the American Southwest, it has been demonstrated that population began to gradually and continually increase sometime between A.D. 700 to 1100. In the Hay Hollow Valley in east-central Arizona, F. Plog (1974) has shown that population began to increase about A.D. 700 and continued to rise until approximately A.D. 1150. Population began to increase by at least A.D. 850 in the Chevelon area and continued to increase until sometime after A.D. 1200 (F. Plog 1974:84). In the Hopi Buttes area of central Arizona, rapid population increase began about A.D. 900 (Gumerman 1975:106). Similarly, Swedlund and Sessions (1976) have demonstrated that population in the northern part of Black Mesa in northeastern Arizona increased beginning about A.D. 800 and continued until abandonment about A.D. 1100 to 1150.

Along with change in population, there was increased expansion into areas that had been only sparsely inhabited previously. As Martin and Plog (1973:327) have argued, the newly colonized areas were probably marginal in terms of agricultural productivity.

> By A.D. 1100 the practice of agriculture was well established on the Colorado Plateau [of northern Arizona]. Those areas that were ideal for the practice of this subsistence technique were filled with people . . . When populations began to grow, and groups budded off from parent

pueblos, the new communities were founded in localities that were less practical for farming than the ones in which the parent pueblos were located. The newly populated areas were marginal with respect to some combination of soil quality, rainfall, the abundance of surface water, and temperature.

Population growth and the colonization of previously sparsely inhabited areas that were marginal for agriculture may have had two important effects on design variation through their effect on mobility and the development of social networks. Mobility may have been reduced, because with increased population density a given social group may not have had free access to as many areas as it had previously [see Ware (1976) for a similar view]. Areas previously exploited were now inhabited and controlled by other individuals. Groups were more localized in the areas they exploited and left debris from their activities. Thus, the ceramic products of a group were not as widely distributed spatially as a result of regular activities and movements of the group itself. These processes thus resulted in a more localized distribution of ceramics.

The reduction in the areas which groups could exploit directly may have led also to the development of larger social networks involving more people. Prior to the population expansion and colonization, the sparsely inhabited areas were probably utilized, if only sporadically or seasonally, for the exploitation of wild resources or for alternative locations for agricultural fields. Ford's (1972a, 1972b) analysis of historic pueblos in the Rio Grande Valley of New Mexico has illustrated the importance of access to a variety of areas of food sources in the American Southwest. Ford (1972b) has shown that rainfall and temperature in the Rio Grande Valley are so variable from one location to another that one agricultural field may be productive while a nearby one may fail. One safeguard against this environmental variability is, as Ford (1972b) has suggested, locating fields in a variety of areas. Prior to the population expansion in the American Southwest prehistorically, populations could attempt to minimize this environmental variability by planting fields in different locations or by gathering wild foods in marginal areas when crops in the more favorable locations failed. This strategy was, however, not possible once these marginal areas had been colonized.

The colonization of marginal areas thus may have resulted in the development of alternative organizational strategies for adapting to a variable environment (Martin and Plog 1973:327–30). R. I. Ford (1972a) and Yengoyan (1972), among others, have noted that social ties between different populations are one means of protecting against an uncertain environment. These social ties, sometimes maintained through formal trade partnerships requiring the movement of goods at set intervals, enable a group to have access to the products of other societies during times of low food productivity. For the American Southwest, Martin and Plog (1973:29) have proposed that such a redistribution system may have been one organizational strategy adopted after the colonization of marginal areas.

This discussion has provided a general argument for why social networks may have expanded as a result of population expansion and the colonization of new areas. Two areas of the American Southwest, the Chevelon and Black Mesa areas, will now be examined in detail in order to discuss why such changes may have occurred within these areas and what evidence there is to suggest that such changes did occur.

The population increase that occurred prehistorically on Black Mesa in northeastern Arizona was just described. Along with the population increase, there was increased settlement in areas where there had been low densities previously (Gumerman, Westfall, and Weed 1972). During the period from A.D. 850 to 950, permanent settlements were primarily concentrated along the major washes. However, resources in the upland areas away from the major washes were exploited by the populations in these settlements. Recent excavation (S. Plog 1977) has demonstrated the presence in the uplands of several small, perhaps seasonally occupied, sites dating to this time period. Analysis of flotation samples taken from these sites has shown agriculture was practiced, although a variety of wild plants, such as grasses, were also being heavily exploited (Ford et al. n.d.).

As population increased, areas more distant from the major washes were increasingly settled. These sites have more structures and more artifactual material, suggesting more permanent habitation and a larger population. Flotation analysis has shown that agricultural products were a major part of the subsistence base (Ford et al. n.d.). In the upland areas, only dry farming or floodwater farming in washes within much smaller catchment basins than those of the major washes was possible. Agricultural productivity in the upland areas was thus more susceptible to variability in rainfall. Also, as a result of the increased colonization, the reduction in mobility discussed earlier occurred. Populations in the lowland areas no longer were able to exploit the upland areas and counter environmental variability through subsistence practices. Populations in the uplands were even more affected by environmental variability because of the marginality of the uplands. Thus, the system as a whole was more susceptible to environmental variability.

Given these changes, evidence also suggests that larger or more cohesive social networks may have developed as an organizational adaptation to environmental variability. Excavation during 1976 (S.

Plog 1977) has shown that the association of masonry storage rooms and jacal habitation rooms with kivas (ceremonial rooms) is not as consistent as past studies (Gumerman, Westfall, and Weed 1972; Phillips 1972) have suggested. Kivas, for example, occur as frequently in the absence of masonry rooms as they do when masonry rooms are present. However, when masonry rooms are present, jacal rooms and a kiva are always present. Moreover, the kivas on sites with masonry rooms tend to be larger and more elaborate than kivas on sites without masonry rooms. Their size does not appear to be correlated with the number of habitation rooms at the site. These data suggest that sites with masonry storage rooms may have been central storage areas for a group of sites. This sharing may have had a religious base, as indicated by the consistent association of storage rooms with kivas and the size and degree of elaboration of the kivas. The association of storage rooms with kivas has been noted in several other areas of the American Southwest and has been explained in this manner (F. Plog 1974). The development of social networks that allowed the pooling of resources among villages would have been one way to counter the susceptibility of these populations to environmental variability.

Changes somewhat similar to those in the Black Mesa area may have occurred in the Chevelon region. In the latter area, the practice of agriculture in both the grassland and juniper pinyon areas may have helped to minimize the effects of environmental variability. The critical limiting factors on agriculture are different in these two vegetation zones. In the grassland area near Winslow, the growing season is long enough for agriculture, with an average of 174 frost-free days (Sellers and Hill 1974:570), but rainfall is very low, with an average of only 188 millimeters (7.4 inches) per year. Rainfall is higher in the pinyon-juniper zone, with an average precipitation of 432 millimeters (17.0 inches) at Heber and 462 millimeters (18.2 inches) at Chevelon Ranger Station (Sellers and Hill 1974:150, 256). However, the growing season is shorter. No figures are given, but Sellers and Hill (174:150) state that at the Chevelon Ranger Station the growing season normally extends from the last week in May to the first week in October, and the data presented indicate that there is an average of at least one day with the minimum temperature below 32 degrees in both June and September. Thus, a maximum growing season of between 120 and 130 days is indicated. At Heber, there is an average of three days in June and two days in September with the minimum temperature below 32 degrees (Sellers and Hill 1974:256), suggesting an average growing season of no more than 115 to 120 days. Hack (1942) reports that Hopi crops need at least 120 frost-free days to mature. Thus, in below average years, some crops at the Heber and Chevelon Ranger Stations would not mature.

If temperature and rainfall covaried prehistorically in the manner that they do today, that is, if temperature and rainfall were inversely correlated, then a given climatic regime would favor either the grassland or the pinyon-juniper area, but not both. Cold, wet years would provide enough rainfall for agriculture in the grassland areas, but would make the growing season too short in the pinyon-juniper area. In contrast, in warmer, drier years the growing season in the pinyon-juniper area would be sufficient, but there would not be enough rainfall for crops in the grassland area. Thus, by planting crops in both areas, prehistoric populations may have insured that some crops matured in any given year.

Given the low population densities in the Chevelon area during the period between approximately A.D. 700 to 1000, it would have been possible for prehistoric populations to employ such a strategy. However, as population increased in the area and the two vegetation zones were permanently occupied, such a strategy would not have been possible and cultural safeguards against environmental variability would have been reduced as the size of the area which a given group had access to decreased. The development of social networks between populations in the grassland and pinyon-juniper zones would have been an alternative organizational strategy. In Chevelon, social ties and economic sharing between the grassland and pinyon-juniper zones would be advantageous because of the different limiting factors on agricultural productivity in the two vegetation zones. I suggest that the evidence of large-scale ceramic exchange between populations in the Winslow area and the Purcell-Larson area indicates that such a social network was developed in the area prehistorically, primarily during the period A.D. 1050 to 1250. As argued before, this exchange was not the result of the differential distribution through space of raw materials for ceramic manufacture. Rather, it may be interpreted as resulting from the establishment and maintenance of social ties between prehistoric populations inhabiting the different environmental zones.

The Black Mesa and Chevelon data in no way demonstrate that larger or more cohesive social networks developed as a result of population increase and the reduction in mobility. The evidence suggests only that such developments were reasonable and may have occurred. Similar changes have been postulated for other areas, however. In the Hope Buttes, Gumerman (1975:111) has proposed that as population increased in the area

> it was essential that there be some social network to insure interaction of the populations of various sites. It is doubtful if these small farming communities were completely autonomous, especially since most of them do not have

kivas. Furthermore, the disparity of environmental factors
in dry farming from year to year and plot to plot would
encourage economic interaction.

He suggests that a site in the area with a high ratio of ceremonial
room to other room types, a large number of storage vessels, and a
great kiva was a special purpose site that was a "socio-religious hub
in a large network of small communities" (1975:112).

To summarize, data from the American Southwest suggest that
there was large scale population increase in the prehistoric Southwest between A.D. 900 to A.D. 1300. The colonization of marginal
environments for agriculture and reduced mobility necessitated the
development of organizational strategies for adaptation to environmental variability. One such strategy that appears to have been
adopted in different areas of the Southwest was the development of
larger, more cohesive social networks to facilitate economic sharing.
The relationship between these changes and temporal and spatial
variation in ceramic designs will now be discussed.

Implications for explanations of design variation

Now that spatial and temporal variation in ceramic designs in the
prehistoric American Southwest have been examined and some associated changes through time in population, mobility, and social networks have been summarized briefly, the implications of these
changes for the theories of stylistic variation must be considered.
That is, the question of whether or not the theories can explain the
stylistic changes must be answered. First, while normative theory can
account for the broad style zones that were present in the American
Southwest, no adequate explanations based on this theoretical position have been developed to account for the wide variation through
time in the size of such zones or the changes in the degree of similarity within zones over time. Moreover, this theory has several important weaknesses. [In-depth criticisms have been made elsewhere
(Binford 1965) that have adequately delineated these weaknesses,
and the reader is referred to them.]

On the other hand, the social interaction–learning theory adequately explains the decrease in the spatial extent of style zones
through time in the American Southwest. The theory would predict
this change, given the decrease through time in the mobility of
groups, the increase in population density, and the development of
stronger social networks. A group thus was interacting most in-
tensely with other groups within a restricted spatial area rather than
physically moving over broad areas, interacting with other groups
with similar patterns of movement. Therefore, it would be expected
that there would be a decrease in the size of style zones.

While the social interaction–learning theory can account for the temporal changes in the extent of style zones, it cannot account for the absolute size of these zones. First, it does not explain the existence of a homogeneous style zone, characterized by the Lino and Kana-a styles as defined by Wasley (1959), over most of northeastern Arizona during the time period from approximately A.D. 400 to 900. Rather, the social interaction–learning theory predicts a clinal pattern through space and decreasing stylistic similarity between sites with increasing distance between them. The rate at which similarity would be expected to decrease with increasing distance would be lower during Basketmaker III and Pueblo I than later time periods, given the lower population density and the increased mobility of populations, but it would not be expected to be so low that there would be a high degree of similarity between areas as distant a Chevelon Canyon and Black Mesa. Second, the social interaction learning theory cannot explain the lack of clinal distributions of designs through space during later time periods when there appear to be a homogeneous distribution of designs through space with style zones. As noted previously, the theory predicts that rooms in single pueblo should be more similar than rooms of different pue los, that sites in the same valley should be more similar than sites different valleys, and so on. However, the studies reviewed earl have shown that such patterns did not occur. One of the prim; test implications of the social interaction–learning theory and emphasis on the individual as the locus of stylistic variation is met. On the basis of the failure of the social interaction–learn theory to explain the spatial extent of style zones in the Ameri Southwest and on the basis of other evidence (S. Plog 1976b suggest that the theory must be rejected.

The evidence concerning stylistic variation through time also (not fit a model of stylistic drift. As noted earlier, Binford (1969 has argued that if drift occurs during demographic increases population budding, "a demonstrable pattern of covariation bet' formal differences" might develop between parent and dau; communities. The fact that population increased and coloniz occurred through time in the American Southwest already has demonstrated. However, rather than stylistic differences develc there was increased stylistic similarity between communities i same area. Thus, stylistic drift cannot account for the chan design variation through both time and space.

The patterned nature of design variation through space an also conflicts with the hypothesis that motor habit variatio account for aspects of design variation. As noted, random va in design frequencies through space and time would be expe the hypothesis were correct. In addition, the Chevelon desigr

sis has shown that some of the attributes such as line widths and distances between lines, which Hill (1977:100) has suggested should be most affected by motor habits, have strong patterns of variation through time, between different vessel forms, and/or between pottery made in different areas. Multivariate analysis of sherds using such attributes would not form clusters representing different individuals, as Hill (1978:254) has suggested, but would form clusters representing sherds of different time periods, of different areas, and of different vessel forms.

In contrast to the inability of the social interaction–learning theory, the model of stylistic drift, and motor habit variation to account for spatial and temporal variation in ceramic designs, I feel that the information exchange theory can explain this variation. First, the spatial extent of style zones is consistent with the theory. The single broad style zone during the period from A.D. 400 to 900 is expected because of the lack of or infrequent occurrence of contact with socially distant individuals; the importance of contact with this category of people has been discussed. The smaller the number of such people, the less efficient "stylistic behavior becomes relative to other communication modes" (Wobst 1977:326). Wobst (1977:326) argues that

> It is not surprising to find that certain aspects of band society material culture show so little evidence of "stylistic" elaboration. Either category 4 [socially distant individuals] is completely lacking in the societies in question so that the functional matrix for stylistic behavior is only weakly developed, or few messages are sufficiently replicative to justify the energy and matter investment required by stylistic communication. As societies increase in size and complexity, more and more aspects of behavior become intertwined with personnel in category 4, and more and more of these behaviors become repetitious and anticipated. It is in the latter societies that stylistic behavior structures important aspects of artifact form.

It is not necessary to consider here the question of whether or not the societies that existed during the period from A.D. 400 to 900 should be characterized as band societies. Given the lack of information from that period on organization, subsistence, and other variables, it is difficult to answer such a question. However, population levels and population density were low during the period (Gumerman 1975, F. Plog 1974, Swedlund and Sessions 1976). It is, thus, possible that population density was so low that stylistic behavior was an inefficient means of communication and that the lack of stylistic behavior was a result. That such was the case cannot be demonstrated. However, the available data are not inconsistent with

Wobst's arguments and they, thus, cannot be used to suggest that the theory is invalid.

In addition to being consistent with the existence of a broad style zone over northeastern Arizona during the period between A.D. 400 to 900, the information exchange theory also is consistent with the reduction in the size of style zones, the extent of style zones during later periods, and the stylistic homogeneity within zones. As noted, Wobst argues (1977:326) that as the size of social networks that individuals participate in increase, the amount of stylistic behavior should increase because of the increased amount of contact with socially distant individuals. Given the evidence already presented for increased population density and the development of larger, spatially more restricted social networks, it would be expected that stylistic behavior would increase within each of the social networks that developed.

The increasing amount of stylistic similarity within style zones may be related to the high degree of visibility of ceramics. For the Chevelon area, it has been demonstrated that a large amount of ceramic exchange occurred in the area, with ceramic vessels being moved over distances of 20 to 50 kilometers. Ceramic exchange may have developed in the Chevelon area and in other areas of the American Southwest as a means of maintaining ties between individuals in the social networks. Thus, ceramics were highly visible, particularly to socially distant individuals. Wobst (1977:330) has proposed that it is specifically those items of material culture most visible to a large group of people that are most likely to carry stylistic messages, particularly messages of social group affiliation. Those artifacts that are most visible will have "specific stylistic forms" with the widest distribution, while those items of material culture that are seen by a small group of people will have stylistic forms that are clinally distributed (Wobst 1977:330). The available evidence on ceramic design variation through space is consistent with this prediction, as noted, inasmuch as there is no clinal distribution of designs in the areas of the Southwest where detailed analyses have been done.

The exchange of ceramics between groups, in addition to increasing the visibility of the designs, also increased the probability that ceramics entered into what Wobst (1977:329) calls "processes of boundary maintenance." He argues (1977:329) that in such cases not only will a given stylistic message be standardized within a group but it will also contrast with similar messages of surrounding groups. Thus, style zones would not be broad but would be somewhat spatially localized. Again, this is not inconsistent with the data on style zones in the prehistoric American Southwest.

This discussion has indicated that the social interaction–learning theory of stylistic behavior is not supported by the available information on design variation in the American Southwest. It cannot explain the spatial extent of style zones through time in the area. In contrast, the available data on ceramic design variation are not inconsistent with the expectations of the information exchange theory developed by Wobst (1977). According to this theory, ceramic designs in the American Southwest after A.D. 900–because of their high degree of visibility and as a result of being one item moved in exchange networks–may have served as a means of communicating information concerning social group affiliation, thus aiding social integration by making social intercourse more predictable and less stressful. This interpretation supports Binford's (1965:206) emphasis on the importance of the social context of manufacture and use of artifacts, particularly those instances in which the contexts are not isomorphic, and his suggestion that stylistic variation may serve "as a conscious expression of between-group solidarity" or may have "symbolized political ties." This aspect of ceramics has not been considered by those who have proposed the social interaction–learning theory of design variability. As noted earlier, they have implicitly assumed that ceramics were manufactured and used by each household. The role of ceramics outside of such a situation has not been considered nor has the possible consequences of these uses on design variation.

While the evidence presented has supported the information exchange theory of stylistic variation, other data from the American Southwest may not support it. First, Wobst (1977:329) has proposed that items of material culture with low visibility will have stylistic forms that are "distributed clinally across the given local group and, very likely, also across its boundaries." It has normally been assumed by archaeologists working in the American Southwest that corrugated pottery was made and used by individual families. It was, according to this assumption, a low visibility item and stylistic attributes would, therefore, according to the information exchange theory, be clinally distributed through space. Although little detailed analysis has been done other than Brunson's (1979) recent study, which does suggest style zones for corrugated pottery for one area of east-central Arizona and west-central New Mexico, I would argue that stylistic attributes of corrugated pottery are very homogeneous throughout most of the Anasazi and Mogollon area in all time periods and are not clinally distributed. Given the validity of these assumptions, this information is inconsistent with the expectations of the information exchange theory. However, we do not know in most cases whether corrugated pottery was made and used by individual families. In at least one area it is known, as has been described earlier, that corrugated pottery was also moved in an exchange system.

Second, the temporal changes in style zones in the American

Southwest could be the result of changes in the mode of ceramic production through time. If there was increasing ceramic exchange within areas, such as was demonstrated in the Chevelon area, or if there was increasing village specialization in pottery manufacturing, as Shepard (1942, 1965) has demonstrated in the Rio Grande Valley, it would also be expected that style zones would decrease through time, design homogeneity within regions would increase, similarity between sites within style zones would increase, and boundaries between style zones would become sharper. The demonstration of large scale ceramic exchange in the Chevelon area and the discussion of previous studies that have also documented frequent ceramic exchange indicate this is a very plausible explanation of changes in design variation through time and space in the American Southwest. Thus, as I have argued throughout this study, we cannot study design variation as if it were largely isolated and unrelated to the *entire* cultural system. The work of Deetz (1965), Whallon (1968), Hill (1970), and Longacre (1970) provided the first change in perspective by arguing stylistic variation was affected by different aspects of social organization. The analysis of ceramic design variation in the Chevelon area has demonstrated that design variation is affected by many other aspects of a cultural system.

Information from other areas

Detailed studies of degrees of intrasite, intersite, and interregional stylistic similarity and homogeneity through time have not been as frequent in areas other than the American Southwest, and my knowledge of such studies is not as broad. Thus, it is not possible to use information from these areas to evaluate the various theories of style in as rigorous a manner as was done for the American Southwest. However, information from two areas is important and will be summarized briefly.

First, I have noted previously that the studies of Whallon (1968, 1969), in particular, and Engelbrecht (1971, 1974, 1979) have not supported the social interaction theory of stylistic variation. These studies of stylistic variation on ceramics from New York State have shown that intrasite homogeneity and intersite similarity do not covary in the manner predicted by that theory. However, the trends of increasing homogeneity within sites and increasing similarity between sites that Whallon (1968, 1969) especially has shown are similar to trends in the American Southwest. In addition, these trends occur at a time when other changes comparable to those in the American Southwest also were occurring. Population was increasing and agricultural intensification was taking place (Whallon 1968:241). In addition, warfare was increasing and Whallon (1968:242–3) suggests that institutionalized methods of controlling intergroup feuding may have evolved. If such was the case, this information also would appear to support an explanation of the changes in stylistic variation based on the information exchange theory. That is, the trends toward intrasite homogeneity and intersite similarity occurred at a time when the size of social networks and contact with socially distant individuals was increasing, causing the value of stylistic variation in communicating group affiliation or in boundary maintenance also to increase. As in the American Southwest, homogeneous style zones with increasingly similar stylistic attributes at sites within the zones may have evolved as a result.

A recent study (Braun 1977) of patterns of stylistic variation in the midwestern United States also has supported the information exchange theory as opposed to the social interaction theory. Braun found that intrasite stylistic homogeneity and regional homogeneity during the Middle and Late Woodland periods covaried directly. As I noted in the first chapter, this is not consistent with the expectations of the social interaction theory. In addition, given evidence that population was increasing in the area with increasing sedentism and a greater need for supralocal integration and cooperation, Braun (1977) has suggested that Wobst's information exchange theory can account for the observed changes in stylistic variation.

Additional considerations

While this discussion has supported the information exchange theory of stylistic variation, two weaknesses of the argument must be pointed out. First, I have concentrated on general stylistic variation in the American Southwest rather than the specific design attributes dealt with in the analysis of the Chevelon ceramics. This was necessitated by the lack of treatment of comparable design attributes or information outside the Chevelon area. For other regions, discussions have often focused on design styles or design elements that are defined by a number of different attributes. The problem with this approach has already been described. In focusing on such design styles, it is clear that certain aspects of design variation have been ignored. For example, different design attributes appear to be distributed on different spatial scales (F. Plog 1977:18). If the colors of painted ceramics are considered, the entire northern half of the American Southwest would have similar ceramics. On the other hand, if the composition of designs is examined, several spatial units within this broad area could be delineated. Thus, as Whallon (1968:223) has argued, "style has many aspects and levels of behavior which may be analytically distinguished and measured." This is important, for as Kintigh (1979) has argued, *different* theories of style may explain variation in different design attributes. The differing spatial scales of attribute distributions noted earlier supports Kintigh's argument.

In addition, variation in some attributes will likely have to be explained by a combination of these theories. For example, Cleland (1972:209) has argued that "if increasing popularity results in more frequent replication of a design motif, we would expect that the design would undergo more rapid style drift resulting from more opportunity for element transfer over relatively short periods of time." Thus, it is possible that the increased rate of design change in the Black Mesa area illustrated in Chapter 7 could be the result of both the increased use of specific designs to convey information concerning social affiliation and the increased drift that Cleland suggests would result from the more frequent replication of these designs.

In short, while I feel the available evidence best supports the information exchange theory of stylistic variation, the case is far from closed. Although stylistic analyses have a long history, we are only beginning to adequately describe and explain stylistic variation. Unfortunately, however, many current studies assume that the causes of stylistic variation are known. Despite frequent criticisms of the equation of stylistic similarity with interaction intensities by myself and others, for example, many recent studies continue to accept this assumption without responding to the criticisms (F. Plog 1977:20). Perhaps the analysis and discussion presented in this study will contribute to understanding the causes of stylistic variation within and between sites – and stylistic variation in general – as well as generate future studies.

References

Aberle, D. F. 1970. Comments. In W. A. Longacre (ed.), *Reconstructing prehistoric pueblo societies*, pp. 214–23. University of New Mexico Press, Albuquerque.

Acker, C. 1973. Soil and environment in the explanation of settlement pattern. Unpublished manuscript, Department of Anthropology, University of California at Los Angeles.

Allen, W. L., and J. B. Richardson. 1971. The reconstruction of kinship from archaeological data: the concepts, the methods, and the feasibility. *American Antiquity* 36:41–53.

Amsden, C. 1936. *An analysis of Hohokam pottery design*. Medallion Papers, no. 23. Gila Pueblo, Globe, Ariz.

Arnold, D. E. 1971. Ethnomineralogy of Ticul, Yucatecan potters: emics and etics. *American Antiquity* 36:20–40.

    1972. Native pottery making in Quinua, Peru. *Anthropos* 67:858–872.

    1975. Ceramic ecology of the Ayacucho Basin, Peru: implications for prehistory. *Current Anthropology* 16:183–205.

Baldwin, S. J. 1975. Archaeological reconstruction of social structure: a critical evaluation of two examples from the Southwest. *Western Canadian Journal of Anthropology* 4:1–22.

Balfet, H. 1965. Ethnographical observations in North Africa and archaeological interpretation: the pottery of the Maghreb. In F. R. Matson (ed.), *Ceramics and man*, pp. 161–77. Aldine, Chicago.

Bannister, B. 1962. The interpretation of tree-ring dates. *American Antiquity* 27:508–14.

Bannister, B., E. Gell, and J. W. Hannah. 1966. *Tree-ring dates from Arizona N–P*. Laboratory of Tree-Ring Research, University of Arizona, Tucson.

Bannister, B., J. W. Hannah, and W. J. Robinson. 1966. *Tree-ring dates from Arizona K*. Laboratory of Tree-Ring Research, University of Arizona, Tucson.

Bannister, B., W. J. Robinson, and R. L. Warren. 1967. *Tree-ring dates from Arizona J*. Laboratory of Tree-Ring Research, University of Arizona, Tucson.

Bannister, B., and W. J. Robinson. 1971. *Tree-ring dates from Arizona U-W*. Laboratory of Tree-Ring Research, University of Arizona, Tucson.

Bareis, C. J., and J. W. Porter. 1965. Megascopic and petrographic analyses of a foreign pottery vessel from the Cahokia site. *American Antiquity* 31:95–101.

Barter, E. R. 1957. Pottery of the Jewett Gap site. In P. S. Martin, J. B.

Rinaldo, and E. R. Barter, *Late Mogollon communities: four sites of the Tularosa phase Western New Mexico*, pp. 106–25. Fieldiana: Anthropology, vol. 49, no. 1. Chicago Natural History Museum, Chicago.

Bartovics, A. F. 1974. The experiment in archaeology: a comparison of two cases. *Journal of Field Archaeology* 1:197–205.

Beals, R. L., G. W. Brainerd, and W. Smith. 1945. *Archaeological studies in northeast Arizona*. University of California Publications in American Archaeology and Ethnology, vol. 44, no. 1. University of California Press, Berkeley.

Bennett, W. C. 1934. *Excavations at Tiahuanaco*. Anthropological Papers of the American Museum of Natural History, vol. 34, pt. 3. American Museum of Natural History, New York.

Bennyhoff, J. A., and R. F. Heizer. 1965. Neutron activation analysis of some Cuicuilco and Teotichuacan pottery: archaeological interpretations of results. *American Antiquity* 30:348–49.

Binford, L. R. 1963. "Red ochre" caches from the Michigan area: a possible case of cultural drift. *Southwestern Journal of Anthropology* 19:89–108.

1964. A consideration of archaeological research design. *American Antiquity* 29:425–41.

1965. Archaeological systematics and the study of culture process. *American Antiquity* 31:203–10.

Bradley, Z. A. 1959. Three prehistoric farm structures at Wupatki National Monument. *Plateau* 32:12–22.

Braun, D. P. 1974. Experimental interpretation of ceramic vessel use on the basis of rim and neck formal attributes. Unpublished manuscript, Department of Anthropology, University of Michigan, Ann Arbor.

1977. Middle Woodland–(Early) Late Woodland social change in the prehistoric central midwestern U.S. Unpublished Ph.D. dissertation, Department of Anthropology, University of Michigan, Ann Arbor.

Brunson, J. L. 1979. Corrugated ceramics as indicators of interaction spheres. Paper presented at the 44th Annual Meeting of the Society for American Archaeology, Vancouver, B.C.

Bunzel, R. L. 1972. *The pueblo potter, a study of creative imagination in primitive art*. Dover Publications, New York.

Carlson, R. L. 1970. *White Mountain redware, a pottery tradition of east-central Arizona and western New Mexico*. Anthropological Papers of the University of Arizona, no. 19. University of Arizona Press, Tucson.

Chagnon, N. 1968. *Yanamamo: the fierce people*. Holt, Rinehart, and Winston, New York.

Chisholm, M. 1968. *Rural settlement and land use*. Aldine, Chicago.

Cibola White Ware Conference. 1958. First Southwestern Ceramic Seminar. Museum of Northern Arizona, Flagstaff.

Clarke, D. L. 1968. *Analytical archaeology*. Methuen, London.

Clay, R. B. 1976. Typological classification, attribute analysis, and lithic variability. *Journal of Field Archaeology* 3:303–11.

Cleland, C. E. 1972. From sacred to profane: style drift in the decoration of Jesuit finger rings. *American Antiquity* 37:202–10.

Clemen, R. T. 1976. Aspects of prehistoric social organization on Black Mesa. In G. J. Gumerman and R. C. Euler (eds.), *Papers on the archaeology of Black Mesa, Arizona*, pp. 113–35. Southern Illinois University Press, Carbondale.

Close, A. E. 1978. The identification of style in lithic artifacts. *World Archaeology* 10:223–37.

Colton, H. S. 1939. *Prehistoric culture units and their relationships in Northern Arizona*. Bulletin 17. Museum of Northern Arizona, Flagstaff.

  1941. Prehistoric trade in the Southwest. *Scientific Monthly* 52:308–19.

  1953. *Potsherds*. The Northern Arizona Society of Science and Art, Flagstaff.

  1955. *Pottery types of the Southwest*. Ceramic series, no. 3B. Museum of Northern Arizona, Flagstaff.

  1973. *Black sand*. Greenwood Press, Westport, Conn.

Colton, H. S., and L. L. Hargrave. 1937. *Handbook of northern Arizona pottery types*. Bulletin 11. Museum of Northern Arizona, Flagstaff.

Colton, M. R. F. 1938. The arts and crafts of the Hopi Indians. *Museum of Northern Arizona Museum Notes* 11:3–24.

Conkey, M. W. 1978. An analysis of design structure: variability among Madalenian engraved bones from northcoastal Spain. Unpublished Ph.D. dissertation, Department of Anthropology, University of Chicago.

Connor, J. 1968. Economic independence and social interaction: related variables in culture change. Unpublished manuscript, Department of Anthropology, Field Museum of Natural History, Chicago.

Cook, T. G. 1970. Social groups and settlement patterns in Basketmaker III. Unpublished master's thesis, Department of Anthropology, University of Chicago.

Cox, N., and E. Mayer. 1972. Analysis of black-on-white sherds from the Chevelon project. Unpublished manuscript, Department of Anthropology, University of California at Los Angeles.

Cronin, C. 1962. An analysis of pottery design elements, indicating possible relationships between three decorated types. In P. S. Martin and others, *Chapters in the prehistory of eastern Arizona*, I, pp. 105–14. Fieldiana: Anthropology, vol. 53. Chicago Natural History Museum, Chicago.

Danson, E. B. 1957. *An archaeological survey of west central New Mexico and east central Arizona*. Papers of the Peabody Museum of Archaeology and Ethnology, vol. 44, no. 1. Peabody Museum of Archaeology and Ethnology, Cambridge, Mass.

Danson, E. B., and R. M. Wallace. 1956. A petrographic study of Gila Polychrome. *American Antiquity* 22:180–82.

Dean, J. S. 1970. *Chronological analysis of Tsegi phase sites in northeastern Arizona*. Paper no. 3. Laboratory of Tree-Ring Research, University of Arizona, Tucson.

  1978. Independent dating in archaeological analysis. *Advances in Archaeological Method and Theory* 1:223–55.

DeAtley, S. P. 1973. A preliminary analysis of patterns of raw material use in plainware ceramics from Chevelon, Arizona. Unpublished master's thesis, Department of Anthropology, University of California at Los Angeles.

Deetz, J. 1965. *The dynamics of stylistic change in Arikara ceramics*. Illinois Studies in Anthropology, no. 4. University of Illinois Press, Urbana.

  1968a Late man in North America: archaeology of European Americans. In B. J. Meggers (ed.), *Anthropological archeology in the Americas*, pp. 121–30. Anthropological Society of Washington, Washington, D.C.

  1968b. Cultural patterning of behavior as reflected by archaeological materials. In K. C. Chang (ed.), *Settlement archaeology*, pp. 31–42. National Press, Palo Alto.

Deetz, J., and E. Dethlefsen. 1965. The doppler effect and archaeology: a consideration of spatial aspects of seriation. *Southwestern Journal of Anthropology* 21:196–206.

  1967. Death's head, cherubs, urn and willow. *Natural History* 76:29–37.

DeGarmo, G. D. 1977. Identification of prehistoric intrasettlement exchange. In T. K. Earle and J. E. Ericson (eds.), *Exchange systems in prehistory*, pp. 153–70. Academic Press, New York.

Dethlefsen, E., and J. Deetz. 1966. Death's heads, cherubs, and willow trees: experimental archaeology in colonial cemeteries. *American Antiquity* 31:502–10.

Deutchman, H. L. 1979. Intra-regional interaction on Black Mesa and among the Kayenta Anasazi: the chemical evidence for prehistoric exchange. Unpublished Ph.D. dissertation, Department of Anthropology, Southern Illinois University, Carbondale.

Dixon, W. J. and F. J. Massey. 1969. *Introduction to statistics*. McGraw-Hill, New York.

Drennan, R. D. 1976. *Fabrica San Jose and Middle Formative society in the Valley of Oaxaca*. Memoirs of the Museum of Anthropology, No. 8, University of Michigan, Ann Arbor.

Earle, T. K. and J. E. Ericson. 1977. *Exchange systems in prehistory*. Academic Press, New York.

Engelbrecht, W. 1971. A stylistic analysis of Iroquois pottery. Unpublished Ph.D. dissertation, Department of Anthropology, University of Michigan, Ann Arbor.

1974. The Iroquois: archaeological patterning on the tribal level. *World Archaeology* 6:52–65.

1979. Inferring prehistoric social and political organization in the northeast. Paper presented at the Conference on Northeast Archaeology, University of Massachusetts, Amherst.

Ericson, J. E. 1977. Egalitarian exchange systems in California. In T. K. Earle and J. E. Ericson (eds.), *Exchange systems in prehistory*, pp. 109–26. Academic Press, New York.

Ericson, J. E., D. Read, and C. Burke. 1972. Research design: the relationship between primary functions and physical properties of ceramic vessels and their implications for ceramic distribution on an archaeological site. *Anthropology UCLA* 3:84–95.

Everett, A. G. 1970. Archae-environmental analysis of the upper Chaco drainage basin, New Mexico. *Year Book of the American Philosophical Society*, pp. 308–10.

Fewkes, Jesse W. 1904. *Two summers work in pueblo ruins*. 22nd Annual Report of the Bureau of American Ethnology, pt. 2.

Flannery, K. V. 1972. The cultural evolution of civilizations. *Annual Review of Ecology and Systematics* 3:399–426.

1976. Analysis of stylistic variation within and between communities. In K. V. Flannery (ed.), *The early Mesoamerican village*, pp. 251–54. Academic Press, New York.

Fontana, B. L., W. J. Robinson, C. W. Cormack, and E. E. Leavitt. 1962. *Papago Indian pottery*. University of Washington Press, Seattle.

Ford, J. A. 1935. *Ceramic decoration sequence at an old Indian village site, near Sicily Island, Louisiana*. Anthropological Study no. 1. Department of Conservation, Louisiana State Geological Survey, New Orleans.

Ford, R. I. 1972a. Barter, gift, or violence: an analysis of Tewa intertribal exchange. In E. Wilmsen (ed.), *Social exchange and interaction*, pp. 21–45. Anthropological Papers of the Museum of Anthropology, no. 51. University of Michigan, Ann Arbor.

1972b. An ecological perspective on the eastern pueblos. In A. Ortiz (ed.), *New perspectives on the pueblos*, pp. 1–17. University of New Mexico Press, Albuquerque.

Ford, R. I., A. Jackson, P. E. Minnis, C. W. Cowan, and J. F. Moore. n.d. Paleoethnobotany on Black Mesa: the 1976 season. Unpublished manuscript, Museum of Anthropology, University of Michigan, Ann Arbor.

Freeman, L., and J. Brown. 1964. Statistical analysis of Carter Ranch pottery. In P. S. Martin and others, *Chapters in the prehistory of eastern Arizona*, II, pp. 126–54. Fieldiana: Anthropology, vol 55. Chicago Natural History Museum, Chicago.

Friedrich, M. 1970. Design structure and social interaction: archaeological implications of an ethnographic analysis. *American Antiquity* 35:332–43.

Fry, R. E., and S. C. Cox. 1974. The structure of ceramic exchange at Tikal, Guatemala. *World Archaeology* 6:209–25.

Gamio, M. 1913. Arqueologia de Atzcapotzalco, D. F., Mexico. Proceedings, Eighteenth International Congress of Americanists, London, pp. 180–7.

Garrett. E. 1976. Personal communication.

Gasser, R. E. n.d. A reappraisal of plant food staples in Anasazi diet. Unpublished manuscript, Museum of Northern Arizona, Flagstaff.

Gerald, R. E. 1975. Drought correlated changes in two prehistoric pueblo communities in southeastern Arizona. Unpublished Ph.D. dissertation, Department of Anthropology, University of Chicago.

Gregory, D. A. 1975. Defining variability in prehistoric settlement morphology. In P. S. Martin and others, *Chapters in the prehistory of eastern Arizona*, IV, pp. 40–6. Fieldiana: Anthropology, vol. 65. Field Museum of Natural History, Chicago.

Gumerman, G. J. 1969. The archaeology of the Hopi Buttes district, Arizona. Unpublished Ph.D. dissertation, Department of Anthropology, University of Arizona, Tucson.

1970. *Black Mesa, survey and excavation in northeastern Arizona, 1968*. Prescott College Studies in Anthropology, no. 2. Prescott College Press, Prescott, Ariz.

1975. Alternative cultural models for demographic change: Southwestern examples. In A. D. Swedlund (ed.), *Population studies in archaeology and biological anthropology: a symposium*, pp. 104–15. Memoir, no. 30. Society for American Archaeology.

Gumerman, G. J., and S. A. Skinner. 1968. A synthesis of the prehistory of the central Little Colorado Valley, Arizona. *American Antiquity* 33:185–99.

Gumerman, G. J., D. Westfall, and C. S. Weed. 1972. *Archaeological investigations on Black Mesa: the 1969–1970 seasons*. Prescott College Studies in Anthropology, no. 4. Prescott College Press, Prescott, Ariz.

Guthe, C. E. 1925. *Pueblo pottery making*. Papers of the Phillips Academy Southwestern Expedition, no. 1. Yale University Press, New Haven.

Hack, J. T. 1942. *The changing physical environment of the Hopi Indians of Arizona*. Papers of the Peabody Museum of American Archaeology and Ethnology, vol. 35, no. 1. Peabody Museum of American Archaeology and Ethnology, Cambridge, Mass.

Hall, E. T. 1971. Two examples of the use of chemical analysis in the solution of archaeological problems. In R. H. Brill (ed.), *Science and archaeology*, pp. 156–64. M.I.T. Press, Cambridge, Mass.

Hanson, J. A. 1975. Stress response in cultural systems: a prehistoric example from east-central Arizona. In P. S. Martin and others, *Chapters in the prehistory of eastern Arizona*, IV, pp. 92–102. Fieldiana: Anthropology, vol. 65. Field Museum of Natural History, Chicago.

Hantman, J., and K. Lightfoot. 1977. The analysis of ceramic designs: a methodology for micro-seriation. Paper presented at the 42nd Annual Meeting of the Society for American Archaeology, New Orleans, Louisiana.

Hantman, J., and S. Plog. 1978. Predicting occupation dates of prehistoric Black Mesa sites: a comparison of methods. Paper presented at the 43rd Annual Meeting of the Society for American Archaeology, Tucson, Ariz.

   n.d. Stylistic change, analytical units, and ceramic dating. Manuscript, in preparation, Department of Anthropology, University of Virginia, Charlottesville.

Harbottle, G., and E. V. Sayre. 1975. Current status of examination of sherds of fine paste ceramics from Altar de Sacrificios and Seibal and their comparison with other Maya fine paste ceramics. In J. A. Sabloff, *Excavations at Seibal: ceramics*, pp. 241–43. Memoirs of the Peabody Museum of Archaeology and Ethnology, vol. 13, no. 2. Peabody Museum of Archaeology and Ethnology, Cambridge, Mass.

Haury, E. W. and L. L. Hargrave. 1931. *Recently dated pueblo ruins in Arizona*. Smithsonian Miscellaneous Collections, vol. 82, no. 11. Smithsonian Institution, Washington, D.C.

Hayano, D. M. 1973. Sorcery, death, proximity and the perception of outgroups: the Tauna Awa of New Guinea. *Ethnology* 12:179–91.

Hayes, A. C. 1964. *The archaeological survey of Wetherill Mesa, Mesa Verde National Park–Colorado*. National Park Service Archeological Research Series, no. 7A. Government Printing Office, Washington, D.C.

Hill, J. N. 1970. *Broken K Pueblo: prehistoric social organization in the American Southwest*. Anthropological Papers of the University of Arizona, no. 18. University of Arizona Press, Tucson.

   1977. Individual variability in ceramics and the study of prehistoric social organization. In J. N. Hill and J. Gunn (eds.), *The individual in prehistory: studies of variability in style in prehistoric technologies*, pp. 55–108. Academic Press, New York.

   1978. Individuals and their artifacts: an experimental study in archaeology. *American Antiquity* 43:245–57.

Hill, J. N., and J. Gunn (eds.). 1977. *The individual in prehistory: studies of variability in style in prehistoric technologies*. Academic Press, New York.

Hodder, Ian. 1974. Regression analysis of some trade and marketing patterns. *World Archaeology* 6:172–89.

   1977. The distribution of material culture items in the Baringo district, western Kenya. *Man* 12:239–69.

Hudson, L. 1975. Prehistoric exchange in the southwest United States: man to man or big man to big man. Unpublished manuscript, Department of Anthropology, University of California at Los Angeles.

Irwin, G. J. 1978a. Pots and entrepots: a study of settlement, trade and the development of economic specialization in Papuan prehistory. *World Archaeology* 9:299–319.

   1978b. The development of Mailu as a specialized trading and manufacturing centre in Papuan prehistory. *Mankind* 11:406–15.

Jack, R. N. 1971. The source of obsidian artifacts in northern Arizona. *Plateau* 43:103–13.

Jennings, J. D. 1966. *Glen Canyon: a summary*. University of Utah Anthropological Papers, no. 81. University of Utah Press, Salt Lake City.

Johnson, A. E., and A. S. Johnson. 1975. *K*-means and temporal variability in Kansas City Hopewell ceramics. *American Antiquity* 40:283–95.

Johnson, G. A. 1973. *Local exchange and early state development in southwestern Iran.* Anthropological Papers of the Museum of Anthropology, no. 51. University of Michigan, Ann Arbor.

Johnson, L. 1972. Problems in "avante garde" archaeology. *American Anthropologist* 74:366–77.

Judd, N. 1954. *The material culture of Pueblo Bonito.* Smithsonian Miscellaneous Collections, vol. 124. Smithsonian Institution Press, Washington D.C.

Karlstrom, T. N. V., G. J. Gumerman, and R. C. Euler. 1976. Paleoenvironmental and cultural correlates in the Black Mesa region. In G. J. Gumerman and R. C. Euler (eds.), *Papers on the archaeology of Black Mesa, Arizona*, pp. 149–61. Southern Illinois University Press, Carbondale.

Kasakoff, A. B., and J. W. Adams, 1977. Spatial location and social organisation: an analysis of Tikopian marriage patterns. *Man* 12:48–64.

Kay, M. 1975. Social distance among central Missouri Hopewell settlements: a first approximation. *American Antiquity* 40:64–71.

Kidder, A. V. 1931. *The pottery of Pecos*, vol. 1. Papers of the Phillips Academy Southwest Expedition, no. 5. Yale University Press, New Haven.

  1972. *An introduction to the study of Southwestern archaeology with a preliminary account of the excavations at Pecos.* Yale University Press, New Haven.

Kidder, A. V., and A. O. Shepard. 1936. *The pottery of Pecos*, vol. 2. Papers of the Phillips Academy Southwest Expedition, no. 7. Yale University Press, New Haven.

Kidder, M. A. and A. V. Kidder. 1917. Notes on the pottery of Pecos. *American Anthropologist* 19:325–60.

Kintigh, K. W. 1979. Social structure, the structure of style, and stylistic patterns in Cibola pottery. Unpublished, preliminary paper, Department of Anthropology, University of Michigan, Ann Arbor.

Kroeber, A. L. 1919. On the principle of order in civilization as exemplified by changes of fashion. *American Anthropologist* 21:235–63.

  1963. *Style and civilizations.* Cornell University Press, Ithaca.

Kroeber, A. L., and M. J. Harner. 1955. *Mohave pottery.* University of California Anthropological Records, vol. 16, no. 1. University of California Press, Berkeley.

Kroeber, A. L., and J. Richardson. 1940. *Three centuries of women's dress fashions: a quantitative analysis.* University of California Anthropological Records, vol. 5, no. 2. University of California Press, Berkeley.

Kushner, G. 1970. A consideration of some processual designs for archaeology as anthropology. *American Antiquity* 35:125–32.

Lathrap, D. W. 1973. The antiquity and importance of long-distance trade relationships in the moist tropics of pre-Columbian South America. *World Archaeology* 5:170–86.

  1975. *Ancient Ecuador: culture, clay, and creativity 3000–300 B. C.* Field Museum of Natural History, Chicago.

LeBlanc, S. A. 1975. Micro-seriation: a method for fine chronological differentiation. *American Antiquity* 40:22–38.

Leone, M. 1968. Neolithic autonomy and social distance. *Science* 162:1150–51.

Lightfoot, K. G. 1978. Casual collecting's impact on archaeological interpretation through regional surface surveys. In F. Plog (ed.), *An analytical approach to cultural resource management: the Little Colorado planning unit*, pp. 91–113. Anthropological Research Papers, no. 13. Department of Anthropology, Arizona State University, Tempe.

Lipe, W. D. 1970. Anasazi communities in the Red Rock Plateau, southeastern Utah. In W. A. Longacre (ed.), *Reconstructing prehistoric pueblo societies*, pp. 84–139. University of New Mexico Press, Albuquerque.

Lischka, J. J. 1975. Broken K revisited: a short discussion of factor analysis. *American Antiquity* 40:220–27.

Longacre, W. A. 1962. Archaeological reconnaissance in eastern Arizona. In P. S. Martin and others, *Chapters in the prehistory of eastern Arizona*, I, pp. 148–67. Fieldiana: Anthropology, vol. 53. Chicago Natural History Museum, Chicago.

 1964a. Sociological implications of the ceramic analysis. In P. S. Martin and others, *Chapters in the prehistory of eastern Arizona*, II, pp. 155–67. Fieldiana: Anthropology, vol. 55. Chicago Natural History Museum, Chicago.

 1964b. The ceramic analysis. In P. S. Martin and others, *Chapters in the prehistory of eastern Arizona*, II, pp. 110–25. Fieldiana: Anthropology, vol. 55. Chicago Natural History Museum, Chicago.

 1966. Changing patterns of social integration: a prehistoric example from the American Southwest. *American Anthropologist* 68:94–102.

 1970. *Archaeology as anthropology: a case study*. Anthropological Papers of the University of Arizona, no. 17. University of Arizona Press, Tucson.

 1974. Kalinga pottery-making: the evolution of a research design. In M. J. Leaf (ed.), *Frontiers of Anthropology*, pp. 51–67. D. Van Nostrand, New York.

 n.d. Kalinga pottery, an ethnoarchaeological study. Unpublished manuscript, Department of Anthropology, University of Arizona, Tucson.

McAllister, S. P., and F. Plog. 1978. Small sites in the Chevelon drainage. In A. E. Ward (ed.), *Limited activity and occupation sites: a collection of conference papers*, pp. 17–23. Contributions to Anthropological Studies no. 1, Center for Anthropological Studies, Albuquerque, N.M.

McGregor, J. C. 1965. *Southwestern archaeology*. University of Illinois Press, Urbana.

McPherron, Alan. 1967. *The Juntunen site and the Late Woodland prehistory of the Upper Great Lakes area*. Anthropological Papers of the Museum of Anthropology, no. 30. University of Michigan, Ann Arbor.

Martin, P. S., W. A. Longacre and J. N. Hill. 1967. *Chapters in the prehistory of eastern Arizona*, III. Fieldiana: Anthropology, vol. 57. Field Museum of Natural History, Chicago.

Martin, P. S., and F. Plog. 1973. *The archaeology of Arizona*. American Museum of Natural History, New York.

Martin, P. S., and J. B. Rinaldo 1951. The Southwestern co-tradition. *Southwestern Journal of Anthropology* 7:215–29.

 1960. *Excavations in the upper Little Colorado drainage eastern Arizona*. Fieldiana: Anthropology, vol. 51, no. 1. Chicago Natural History Museum, Chicago.

Martin, P. S., J. B. Rinaldo, and W. A. Longacre. 1960. *Documentation for some late Mogollon sites in the upper Colorado drainage, eastern Arizona*. Archives of Archaeology, no. 6. University of Wisconsin Press, Madison.

 1961a. *Documentation for prehistoric investigations in the upper Little Colorado drainage, eastern Arizona*. Archives of Archaeology, no. 13. University of Wisconsin Press, Madison.

 1961b. *Mineral Creek site and Hooper Ranch Pueblo Eastern Arizona*. Fieldiana: Anthropology, vol. 52. Chicago Natural History Museum, Chicago.

1964. *Documentation for prehistory of Arizona*, II. Archives of Archaeology, no. 24. University of Wisconsin Press, Madison.

Martin, P. S., J. B. Rinaldo, W. A. Longacre, C. Cronin, L. G. Freeman, and J. Schoenwetter. 1962. *Chapters in the prehistory of eastern Arizona*, I. Fieldiana: Anthropology, vol. 53. Chicago Natural History Museum, Chicago.

Martin, P. S., J. B. Rinaldo, W. A. Longacre, L. G. Freeman, J. A. Brown, R. H. Hevly, and M. E. Cooley. 1964. *Chapters in the prehistory of eastern Arizona*, II. Fieldiana: Anthropology, vol. 55. Chicago Natural History Museum, Chicago.

Matson, F. R. 1965. *Ceramics and man*. Viking Fund Publications in Anthropology, no. 41. Aldine, Chicago.

Menzel, D. 1976. *Pottery style and society in ancient Peru*. University of California Press, Berkeley.

Menzel, D., J. H. Rowe, and L. E. Dawson. 1964. *The Paracas pottery of Ica: a study in style and time*. University of California Publications in American Archaeology and Ethnology, vol. 50. University of California Press, Berkeley.

Morris, E. H. 1939. *Archaeological studies in the La Plata district*. Publication no. 519. Carnegie Institute of Washington, Washington D.C.

Muller, J. 1973. *Structural studies of art styles*. Ninth International Congress of Anthropological and Ethnological Sciences, Chicago.

Myers, T. P. 1975. Isolation and ceramic change: a case from the Ucayali River, Peru. *World Archaeology* 7:333–51.

Nelson, N. C. 1916. Chronology of the Tano ruins, New Mexico. *American Anthropologist* 18:159–80.

Olsson, G. 1965. Distance and human interaction: a migration study. *Geografiska Annaler* 47:3–43.

Overstreet, D. F. 1978. Oneonta settlement patterns in eastern Wisconsin: some considerations of time and space. In B. D. Smith (ed.), *Mississippian settlement patterns*, pp. 21–52. Academic Press, New York.

Peacock, D. P. S. 1970. The scientific study of ancient ceramics: a review. *World Archaeology* 1:375–89.

Perlman, I., and F. Asaro. 1971. Pottery analysis by neutron activation. In R. H. Brill (ed.), *Science and archaeology*, M.I.T. Press, Cambridge, Mass.

Phillips, D. A. 1972. Social implications of settlement distribution on Black Mesa. In G. J. Gumerman, D. Westfall, and C. S. Weed, *Archaeological Investigations on Black Mesa, the 1969–1970 Seasons*, pp. 199–210. Prescott College Studies in Anthropology, no. 4. Prescott College Press, Prescott, Ariz.

Pires-Ferreira, J. 1973. Formative Mesoamerican exchange networks. Unpublished Ph.D. dissertation, Department of Anthropology, University of Michigan, Ann Arbor.

Plog, F. 1972. Explaining variability in the distribution of prehistoric settlements. Unpublished manuscript, Department of Anthropology, Arizona State University, Tempe.

1974. Settlement patterns and social history. In M. J. Leaf (ed.), *Frontiers of anthropology*, pp. 69–91. D. Van Nostrand, New York.

1977. Archaeology and the individual. In J. N. Hill, and J. Gunn (eds.), *The individual in prehistory: studies of variability in style and prehistoric technologies*, pp. 13–21. Academic Press, New York.

1978. An analysis of variability in site locations in the Chevelon drainage, Arizona. In R. C. Euler, and G. J. Gumerman (eds.), *Investigations of the Southwestern Anthropological Research Group: the proceedings of 1976 conference*, pp. 53–71. Museum of Northern Arizona, Flagstaff.

Plog, F., R. Effland, and D. Green. 1978. Inferences using the SARG data bank. In R. C. Euler and G. J. Gumerman (eds.), *Investigations of the Southwestern Anthropological Research Group: the proceedings of the 1976 conference*, pp. 139–48. Museum of Northern Arizona, Flagstaff.

Plog, S. 1976a. The inference of prehistoric social organization from ceramic design variability. *Michigan Discussions in Anthropology* 1:1–47.

1976b. Measurement of prehistoric interaction between communities. In K. V. Flannery (ed.), *The early Mesoamerican village*, pp. 255–72. Academic Press, New York.

1976c Relative efficiencies of sampling techniques for archaeological surveys. In K. V. Flannery (ed.), *The early Mesoamerican village*, pp. 136–58. Academic Press, New York.

1978. Social interaction and stylistic similarity: a reanalysis. *Advances in Archaeological Method and Theory* 1:143–82.

Plog, S. (ed.). 1977. *Excavation on Black Mesa, 1976: a preliminary report.* Archaeological Service Report, no. 50. University Museum, Southern Illinois University, Carbondale.

Plog, S., F. Plog, and W. Wait. 1978. Decision making in modern surveys. *Advances in Archaeological Method and Theory* 1:383–421.

Pollnac, R. B., and R. M. Rowlett. 1977. Community and supracommunity within the Marne culture: a stylistic analysis. In D. Ingersoll, J. E. Yellen, and W. Macdonald (eds.), *Experimental archeology*, pp. 167–90. Columbia University Press, New York.

Porter, James. 1976. Personal communication.

Pyne, N. M. 1976. The fire-serpent and were-jaguar in Formative Oaxaca: a contingency table analysis. In K. V. Flannery, (ed.), *The early Mesoamerican village*, pp. 272–82. Academic Press, New York.

Rands, R. L. 1961. Elaboration and invention in ceramic traditions. *American Antiquity* 26: 331–40.

Rappaport, R. A. 1968. *Pigs for the ancestors.* Yale University Press, New Haven.

Read, D. W. 1974. Some comments on typologies in archaeology and an outline of a methodology. *American Antiquity* 39:216–42.

Redman, C. L. 1977. The "analytical individual" and prehistoric style variability. In J. N. Hill and J. Gunn (eds.), *The individual in prehistory: studies of variability in style and prehistoric technologies*, pp. 41–53. Academic Press, New York.

1978. Multivariate artifact analysis: a basis for multidimensional interpretations. In C. L. Redman (ed.), *Social archaelogy: beyond subsistence and dating*, pp. 159–92. Academic Press, New York.

Reher, C. A. 1977. Settlement and subsistence along the lower Chaco River. In C. A. Reher (ed.), *Settlement and subsistence along the lower Chaco River: the CGP survey*, pp. 7–111. University of New Mexico Press, Albuquerque.

Renfrew, C. 1969. Trade and culture process in European prehistory. *Current Anthropology* 10:151–69.

Rinaldo, J. B. 1959. *Foote Canyon Pueblo.* Fieldiana: Anthropology, vol. 49, no. 2. Chicago Natural History Museum, Chicago.

Roberts, F. H. H. 1929. *Shabik'eschee village, a late Basket Maker site in the*

Chaco Canyon, New Mexico. Bureau of American Ethnology, bulletin 92. Government Printing Office, Washington, D.C.

1931. *The ruins at Kiatuthlana.* Bureau of American Ethnology, bulletin 100. Government Printing Office, Washington, D.C.

Rogers, M. W. 1936. *Yuman pottery making.* San Diego Museum Papers, no. 2. San Diego Museum, San Diego.

Rohn, A. H. 1971. *Mug House, Mesa Verde National Park, Colorado.* National Park Service Archaeological Series, no. 7D. Government Printing Office, Washington, D.C.

Rouse, I. 1960. The classification of artifacts in archaeology. *American Antiquity* 25:313–23.

1965. Caribbean ceramics: a study in method and theory. In F. R. Matson, (ed.), *Ceramics and man,* pp. 88–103. Aldine, Chicago.

Rowe, J. H. 1959. Archaeological dating and culture process. *Southwestern Journal of Anthropology* 15:317–24.

Rubertone, P. E. 1978. Social organization in an Islamic town: a behavioral explanation of ceramic variability. Unpublished Ph.D. dissertation, Department of Anthropology, State University of New York, Binghamton.

Russell, F. 1975. *The Pima Indians.* University of Arizona Press, Tucson.

Sabloff, J. A., and C. C. Lamberg-Karlovsky (eds.). 1975. *Ancient civilization and trade.* University of New Mexico Press, Albuquerque.

Sahlins, M. 1972. *Stone age economics.* Aldine-Atherton, Chicago.

Sayre, E. V., and L. Chan. 1971. High-resolution gamma ray spectroscopic analyses of fine orange pottery. In R. H. Brill (ed.), *Science in archaeology,* pp. 165–79. M.I.T. Press, Cambridge, Mass.

Schaefer, P. D. 1969. Prehistoric trade in the Southwest and the distribution of Pueblo IV Hopi Jeddito Black-on-yellow. *Kroeber Anthropological Papers* 41:54–77.

Schiffer, M. B. 1972. Archaelogical context and systemic context. *American Antiquity* 37:156–65.

1976. *Behavioral archeology.* Academic Press, New York.

Sellers, W. D., and R. H. Hill (eds.). 1974. *Arizona climate 1931–1972.* University of Arizona Press, Tucson.

Shepard, A. O. 1939. Technology of La Plata pottery. In E. H. Morris, *Archeological studies in the La Plata district,* pp. 249–287. Publication no. 519. Carnegie Institute of Washington, Washington, D.C.

1942. *Rio Grande glaze paint ware.* Contributions to American Anthropology and History, vol. 7, no. 39. Carnegie Institute of Washington, Washington, D.C.

1948. *Plumbate–a Mesoamerican trade ware.* Publication no. 573. Carnegie Institute of Washington, Washington, D.C.

1953. Notes on color and paste composition. In F. Wendorf, *Archaeological studies in the Petrified Forest National Monument,* pp. 177–93. Bulletin 27. Museum of Northern Arizona, Flagstaff.

1958. *The symmetry of abstract design with special reference to ceramic decoration.* Publication no. 574. Carnegie Institute of Washington, Washington, D.C.

1965. Rio Grande glaze-paint pottery: a test of petrographic analysis. In F. R. Matson (ed.), *Ceramics and man,* pp. 62–87. Viking Fund Publications in Anthropology, no. 41. Aldine, Chicago.

1971. *Ceramics for the archaeologist.* Publication no. 609. Carnegie Institute of Washington, Washington, D.C.

Sidrys, R. 1977. Mass-distance measures for the Maya obsidian trade. In T.

K. Earle and J. E. Ericson (eds.), *Exchange systems in prehistory*, pp. 91–107. Academic Press, New York.

Smith, D. B. 1978. *Prehistoric patterns of human behavior*. Academic Press, New York.

Snarkis, M. J. 1976. Stratigraphic excavations in the eastern lowlands of Costa Rica. *American Antiquity* 41:342–53.

Specht, J. 1974. Of Menak and men: trade and the distribution of resources on Buka Island, Papua New Guinea. *Ethnology* 13:225–37.

Spier, L. 1970. *Yuman tribes of the Gila River*. University of Chicago Press, Chicago.

Stanislawski, M. B. 1969. The ethno-archaeology of Hopi pottery making. *Plateau* 42:27–33.

1973. Review of Archaeology as anthropology: a case study. *American Antiquity* 38:117–21.

Stanislawski, M. B., and B. S. Stanislawski, 1974. Hopi and Hopi-Tewa ceramic tradition networks. Paper presented at the 73rd Annual Meeting of the American Anthropological Association, Mexico City.

Stiger, M. A. 1977. Anasazi diet: the coprolite evidence. Unpublished master's thesis, Department of Anthropology, University of Colorado, Boulder.

Strong, W. D., and C. Evans. 1952. *Cultural stratigraphy in the Viru Valley, northern Peru*. Columbia University Press, New York.

Swedlund, A. C., and S. E. Sessions. 1976. A development model of prehistoric population growth on Black Mesa, northeastern Arizona. In G. J. Gumerman and R. C. Euler (eds.), *Papers on the archaeology of Black Mesa, Arizona*, pp. 136–48. Southern Illinois University Press, Carbondale.

Thomas, H. L., R. M. Rowlett, and E. S. J. Rowlett. 1976. Excavations on the titelberg, Luxembourg. *Journal of Field Archaeology* 3:241–59.

Thompson, R. H. 1958. *Modern Yucatecan Maya pottery making*. Memoirs of the Society for American Archaeology, no. 15. Society for American Archaeology, Salt Lake City.

Tschopik, H. 1941. *Navaho pottery making, an inquiry into the affinities of Navaho painted pottery*. Papers of the Peabody Museum of American Archaeology and Ethnology, vol. 17, no. 1. Peabody Museum of Amer-·icna Archaeology and Ethnology, Cambridge, Mass.

1950. An Andean ceramic tradition in historical perspective. *American Antiquity* 15:196–218.

Tuggle, H. D. 1979. Prehistoric community relations in east-central Arizona. Unpublished Ph.D. dissertation, Department of Anthropology, University of Arizona, Tucson.

Vaillant, G. C. 1930. *Excavations at Zacatenco*. Anthropological Papers of the American Museum of Natural History, vol. 32, pt. 1. American Museum of Natural History, New York.

1931. *Excavations at Ticoman*. Anthropological Papers of the American Museum of Natural History, vol. 32, pt. 2. American Museum of Natural History, New York.

Vivian, R. Gwinn. 1969. Archaeological salvage on the Pinedale and Clay Springs' sections, Payson-Showlow highway, State Route 160, a preliminary report. Unpublished manuscript, Arizona State Museum, University of Arizona, Tucson.

Voorhies, B. 1973. Possible social factors in the exchange system of the prehistoric Maya. *American Antiquity* 38:486–89.

Voss, J. S. 1976. Tribal emergence in the Neolithic of northwestern Europe. Proposal to the National Science Foundation, Washington, D.C.

Wait, W. n.d. Chemical distance between types and sites, a preliminary report. Unpublished manuscript, Department of Anthropology, State University of New York at Binghamton.

Ware, J. A. 1976. Black Mesa: a model of culture change. Unpublished manuscript, Department of Anthropology, Southern Illinois University, Carbondale.

Warren, H. 1969. Tonque, one pueblo's glaze pottery industry dominated middle Rio Grande commerce. *El Palacio* 76:36–42.

Washburn, D. K. 1977. *A symmetry analysis of upper Gila area ceramic design*. Papers of the Peabody Museum of Archaeology and Ethnology, vol. 68. Peabody Museum of Archaeology and Ethnology, Cambridge, Mass.

1978. A symmetry classification of pueblo ceramic design. In P. Grebinger (ed.), *Discovering past behavior: experiments in the archaeology of the American Southwest*. Gordon and Breach, New York.

Washburn, D. K., and R. G. Matson, 1980. Use of multidimensional scaling to display sensitivity of structural pattern analysis to spatial and chronological change: examples from Anasazi prehistory. Unpublished manuscript, Department of Anthropology, California Academy of Sciences.

Wasley, W. W. 1959. Cultural implications of style trends in Southwestern prehistoric pottery. Unpublished Ph.D. dissertation, Department of Anthropology, University of Arizona, Tucson.

Weigand, P. C., G. Harbottle, and E. V. Sayre. 1977. Turquoise exchange and source analysis: Mesoamerica and the Southwestern United States. In T. K. Earle and J. E. Ericson (eds.), *Exchange systems in prehistory,* pp. 15–34. Academic Press, New York.

Whallon, R. 1968. Investigations of late prehistoric social organization in New York State. In S. R. Binford and L. R. Binford (eds.), *New perspectives in archeology,* pp. 223–44. Aldine, Chicago.

1969. *Reflections on social interaction in Owasco ceramic decoration.* Bulletins 27 and 28:15. Eastern States Archaeological Federation, Andover, Mass.

Whittlesey, S. M. 1974. Identification of imported ceramics through functional analysis of attributes. *The Kiva* 40:101–12.

Wiley, C. 1971. Social interaction and economic exchange in the Hay Hollow Valley 900–1200 A.D. Unpublished manuscript, Department of Anthropology, Field Museum of Natural History, Chicago.

Willey, G. R., and P. Phillips. 1958. *Method and theory in American archaeology.* University of Chicago Press, Chicago.

Wilmsen, E. N. 1973. Interaction, spacing behavior, and the organization of hunting bands. *Journal of Anthropological Research* 29:1–31.

Wilson, J. P. 1969. The Sinagua and their neighbors. Unpublished Ph.D. dissertation, Department of Anthropology, Harvard University, Cambridge, Mass.

Windes, T. C. 1977. Typology and technology of Anasazi ceramics. In A. Reher (ed.), *Settlement and subsistence along the lower Chaco River,* pp. 279–370. University of New Mexico Press, Albuquerque.

Wobst, H. M. 1977. Stylistic behavior and information exchange. In C. E. Cleland (ed.), *Papers for the director: research essays in honor of James B. Griffin,* pp. 317–42. Anthropological Papers of the Museum of Anthropolgy, no. 61. University of Michigan, Ann Arbor.

Wright, H., and M. Zeder. 1977. The simulation of a linear exchange system under equilibrium conditions. In T. K. Earle and J. E. Ericson, (eds.), *Exchange systems in prehistory,* pp. 233–53. Academic Press, New York.

Yengoyan, A. A. 1972. Ritual and exchange in aboriginal Australia: An adaptive interpretation of male initiation rites. In E. N. Wilmsen (ed.), *Social exchange and interaction,* pp. 5–9. Anthropological Papers of the Museum of Anthropology, no. 46. University of Michigan, Ann Arbor.

Zipf, G. 1949. Human behavior and the principle of least effort. Addison-Wesley, Cambridge, Mass.

Index

American Southwest
  population levels and mobility,
    129–30, 131, 133, 134
  prehistory of, 26–8
  social networks, 130–1, 131–2,
    133–4
  spatial variation in ceramic de-
    signs, 122–6
  temporal variation in ceramic de-
    signs, 126–9
Amsden, C., 18
Arnold, D. E., 87, 88
artifact form, *see* form of artifact
attributes
  decisions, hierarchy, 41–2, 47, 53
  on different vessel forms, 17–18,
    98, 112–13
  primary versus secondary forms,
    47–9
  rates of change, 108–11
  substitutability, 41–2, 42–3
Aymara, 84, 85

Balfet, H., 76
Binford, L. R., 15, 115–16, 120–1
Black Mesa, 60, 77–8, 82, 108–9,
  129, 131–2
Black Mesa style, 127
Braun, D. P., 11, 85, 90, 117–18, 140
Broken K Pueblo, 11, 14, 43, 44,
  62, 107, 114, 123
Bunzel, R. K., 13, 17

Carlson, R. L., 46, 47–8, 49, 107
Carter Ranch Site, 7, 8, 11, 40, 55–
  6, 74, 107, 114, 123

ceramic vessels
  covariation of decoration and
    form, 90–2
  covariation of temper and deco-
    ration, 89–90
  covariation of temper and form,
    92–3
  ethnographic information, 83–8
  functional types, 93–4
Chaco Canyon, 58–60
Chagnon, N., 21–2
Chevelon Canyon
  archaeological research in, 28–9
  culture history, 29
  dating of sites, 32–3
  functional analysis of ceramics,
    89–95
  location and environmental char-
    acteristics, 28, 132–3
  population estimates, 129
  settlement distribution, 31–2
  site density and size, 31–2, 78–
    9
  social networks, 133
  see also Purcell-Larson
Chontal, 87
Cibola area, 75, 108, 123, 125
Cibola White Ware, 26, 29, 32, 33,
  49–50, 63, 65–6
  see also PGM
Clarke, D. L., 41
Clear Creek, 65, 79–80
Cleland, C. E., 121, 141
Colton, H. M., 63, 127
Connor, J., 11
Cronin, C., 22–3, 124

orifice diameter of vessels, 72
spatial distribution, 63, 65
vessel forms, 72
see also Cibola White Ware
Pima, 84, 85, 86, 87
Pinedale area
  ceramic assemblages on sites, 95–6
  site size, 35, 80–1
  surface collections, 38
  survey strategy, 35–8
Plog, F., 8, 23, 31, 89, 129–30
Pueblo Bonito, 59–60
Puerco style, 107, 127
Purcell-Larson area
  archaeological research in, 28
  artifact density on sites, 77–8
  ceramic assemblages on sites, 95–6
  dating of sites, 99–105
  excavations, 38–9
  functional analysis of ceramics, 89–95
  site size and density, 32, 77
  subsistence-settlement system, 76–8, 81–2, 96
  surface collections, 38
  see also Chevelon Canyon
PSO, 32, 33, 34, 75
see also Tusayan White Ware

Rappaport, R. A., 20–1
Read, D. W., 33–4
Redman, C. L., 44, 75–6, 108, 123
Reserve Black-on-white, 107, 108
Rio Grande Valley, 56–7, 130
Roberts, F. H. H., 127
Rogers, M. W., 84
Russell, F., 84, 87–88

St. Johns Black-on-red, 98, 123
St. Johns Polychrome, 123
Salmon area, 7, 125
San Ildefonso, 86, 87
Schiffer, M. B., 16
Shepard, A. O., 54, 56–7, 58–60
Skinner, S. A., 63
Snowflake Black-on-white, 33, 50, 55–6, 63–4, 74

social interaction theory, 1–3, 5–12, 115, 116–17, 120, 134
social networks, 130–1, 131–2, 133–4
Southwest, *see* American Southwest
Spier, L., 84
SShO, 32, 33, 34
  chemical composition, 68–9
  design analysis of, 50–3
  design attributes, 70, 112
  exchange of, 71, 73, 74, 75
  frequency variation through time, 73–4
  mineral composition, 65–7
  orifice diameter of vessels, 72
  spatial distribution, 63–5
  vessel forms, 72
  see also Little Colorado White Ware
Stanislawski, B. S., 5
Stanislawski, M. B., 5
stylistic drift, 115, 116, 121, 135, 141
stylistic variation
  American Southwest, 122–9
  ceramic vessel form, 17–19
  exchange and, 19–22
  explanation of, 12, 13, 24–5
  importance of studies, 3–4
  intersite/intrasite similarities, 2–3
  Midwestern United States, 140
  New York State, 139–40
  oversimplification of studies, 13–14
  space change, 2–3, 5–12, 122–6
  subsistence-settlement systems and, 14–17, 97–8
  theories of, 115–21, 134–40
  time change, 1, 4–5, 22–4, 105–11, 112, 114, 126–9
subsistence-settlement systems, 14–19, 97–8

tree-ring dating, 99–104
Tschopik, H., 84
Tuggle, H. D., 42, 128
Tularosa Black-on-white, 50, 107, 108
Tularosa style, 107